THE EVERYDAY JOURNEY

FROM DEPRESSION TO LIGHT

BRENDA DONAHUE

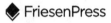 FriesenPress

Suite 300 - 990 Fort St
Victoria, BC, V8V 3K2
Canada

www.friesenpress.com

I would like to thank Megan Cullerton, Bob Donahue, and Jackie Bolger for editing the manuscript and working with me on simplifying and clarifying my ideas.

ISBN
978-1-5255-7266-1 (Hardcover)
978-1-5255-7267-8 (Paperback)
978-1-5255-7268-5 (eBook)

1. SELF-HELP, DEPRESSION

Distributed to the trade by The Ingram Book Company

Table of Contents

INTRODUCTION

Life is wonderful, beautiful, and also very hard. Sometimes the hard overcomes the beautiful, and suffering becomes the order of the day. Sometimes suffering extends itself into ongoing depression. Depression is like a blanket that dims our perceptions, squeezing the vivid into the dull, shutting out beauty and joy. It is like a little death that does not end. Depression depletes our energy, making it almost impossible to hope for anything better. Depression is held in place through repeated enactments of what I call drama, which is acted out internally or externally.

Drama is structured from our innate human abilities: emotional, physical, mental, spiritual, and sexual. Each of these abilities carries energy. When one or more of these abilities are numbed or depleted, we suffer from depression. Drama is a repetitive pattern of reaction to life events, and often we are not aware that we are caught within it. This pattern contains negative elements of resentment, fear, shame, guilt, and anger toward others or toward ourselves.

This book presents multiple viewpoints into depression and drama to help readers understand where they are being held hostage. Understanding brings awareness, and when we are aware, we can make changes that increase our life energy, enabling us to create a richer, fuller life. Our energy vibrates in harmony with nature. All life is moving, changing, and transforming. Think of how many times you have seen a flower change and how these changes transform the flower from bud, to bloom, to death, to decay, and back into bud. We are like that flower, but when we are depressed we are stuck in death, and the transformations necessary for us to develop in wisdom and beauty cannot take place.

This book uses stories, exercises, and examples to amplify the experience of depression and create multiple perspectives into how depression is formed and how it is healed. A questionnaire is provided that will help readers identify parts of the drama in order to step back and observe it. We cannot change what we are not aware of.

This book also presents life skills that readers can use to increase life energy, so they can step out of the drama by raising their life energy and begin the process of transformation. These skills are breath work, chanting, physical movement, and sexual exercises. The last exercise provided is a ceremony of forgiveness of oneself and others.

Sometimes depression can be so debilitating that even using the life skills for transformation are too much effort. If this is the case for you, please seek professional help.

As depression begins to lift, the Light enters our being. There are many names for the Light, and sometimes we argue over the names. The name is not the experience. Please use the ideas and skills that work for you and then discard the rest.

CHAPTER ONE

The Drama

A drama presents real aspects of life in a story that is acted out on stage, in a movie, or on television. Drama can also be played out in real life as the product of someone's overreaction to certain life events. In this book, I employ the latter definition. This kind of drama is always linked with depression. Depression is a psychological mood that causes real suffering. It is as if a dark cloud is surrounding a person that distorts perceptions, diminishes pleasure, and slows down their thought processes. A person who is depressed has recurrent thoughts of death that come from feelings of worthlessness or inappropriate guilt. The person lacks the ability to concentrate and has difficulty making decisions. The person suffering from depression will feel tired all the time and withdraw from relationships by pushing people away or by being irritable and difficult to deal with. The body is affected through weight gain or loss, and physical movement is diminished.

When we are suffering from depression, we are always involved in some sort of drama. This drama operates outside of our awareness. It may take place internally through rumination, or it may take place in our everyday life. We may be familiar with parts of the drama, but we are not aware of its totality. The drama is repetitive and ongoing. It is held together by an emotional theme that is like the background music that is played during a movie.

Every drama has the same central roles: the victim, the tyrant, and the someone or something that saves the day.[1]

A drama can be enacted internally or externally, and it comes with a level of intensity. The higher the intensity of the drama, the closer to death it is. The drama is held in place by depression. Human beings have five aspects: emotional, physical, mental, spiritual, and sexual. When a person is suffering from depression, the energy belonging to one of these five aspects is depleted, and the drama compensates for that lack. Emotions can be blocked or transformed into something else.

The idea of blocked emotions is easy to understand because the tone of voice of the person is flat, and he or she may be slow to respond or non-responsive. Transformation of the emotions is more difficult to understand because the emotions are layered. Fear or sadness can become anger, and anger can become guilt. The layering of emotion leads to indecisiveness and confusion. Depression manifests itself in the body by making it harder for the person to move around. It can lead to weight gain or weight loss. Mentally, the person has repetitive thoughts of doom and death. Spiritually, the person is joyless and cut off from light and love. Sexually, the person may lack any desire for sex, or the person may become hypersexual. All depression affects relationships, and all depression is accompanied by drama, parts of which are unconscious. Because of this lack of awareness, persons suffering from depression are not aware of the drama and keep acting it out over and over. When the drama is triggered, the emotional theme takes over, and the person is no longer present in the here and now. He or she is locked into the drama. Thinking and the ability to observe accurately are not operating at full capacity. Emotions override thinking and influence the way we relate to ourselves and others. Being in drama depletes our life energy. The more we live in drama, the less life energy we have.

As mentioned, one of the roles in every drama is that of tyrant. Inner tyrants include fear, guilt, attachments, expectations (issues about

---

1   Stephen Karpman, MD, developed this idea in his book A Game Free Life (1968).

how we think things will turn out and manipulating them to go in that direction), dependencies, shame, competition, self-pity, and self-importance. Each of these inner tyrants can hold us hostage and lock us into depression.

If one of these tyrants is holding you hostage, use your journal to help you track it down, see how and when it operates. Make friends with it. Name it. Then try to understand the hold it has over you. Respect it, for it is a teacher. Once you understand it, treat it with compassion, and let it go. (This process is discussed more fully in chapter nine.)

In the same way, we encounter several outer tyrants each day. Sometimes an outer tyrant can be as petty as the person sitting in front of us at the movies who keeps crackling candy wrappers while discussing the merits of the movie with the person sitting next to him or her. Sometimes a tyrant can have the power of life or death over us. Sometimes it is someone we love. All tyrants lower our life energy.

The following story is about a woman in her late sixties who came to me for help because she was depressed. She talked about a nightmare she had been having since she was ten years old.

"There is a huge train coming down the tracks," she said as she recalled the dream. "My foot is caught in the rail, and I am sure I'm going to die. At the very last moment, I wiggle out of my shoe and barely miss being killed. I wake up curled in a ball and drenched in sweat."

As we sat together with her dream and the images in it, she became aware of the terror she felt much of the time in her waking life, and she realized that the terror from her dream was often making choices for her. All her life she had experienced authority as "train-like" and wiggled out of orders given to her by those she perceived as authorities. As we sat with the dream image, she became aware of how close she felt to death with that train coming right at her.

The woman was a sixty-five-year-old nun who had spent her life teaching children and being the principal of several schools. She could recall many times that she had "wiggled" out of a sticky situation with an authority figure to avoid conflict. As we discussed it, she spoke of the shame she felt for having lived much of her life in fear and avoidance.

The image of the locomotive coming toward her was terrifying and reminded her that death was coming closer and closer, making her deeply aware of how she truly felt about it. Her comments were derogatory toward herself. She was a religious person, so how could she be so afraid of death? We sat together in silence.

We sat together in silence, the emotions too powerful to be put into words, so she decided to use paper and colored markers to express what she was experiencing. She showed great courage, and when she finally turned and faced her lifelong terror of being annihilated, it no longer had any power over her. When she was able to forgive herself for acting out of terror and realized this was what the dream was calling her to do, her work with me was finished.

Three years after completing her work with me, she died peacefully in her sleep. She suffered a debilitating stroke, and those who cared for her wrote me to tell me that she was peaceful and joyful until the end.

When you are enacting your drama, you are out of the reality of what is really going on, and what is worse, you don't know it. Before this woman came for analysis, she did not understand that many of the choices she made when she was held within her drama hurt her and others. The result of her lack of awareness was depression. Her depression was held in place because the real problem (the enormous train) was blocked from her awareness. When she finally faced the "terrible thing," her depression dropped away, setting her free.

We humans have four enemies: fear, guilt, old age, and death. To make friends with death, we must erase our personal history. Erasing our personal history is letting go of the negative chatter that keeps our minds clouded. As we erase, we develop a sense of inner silence, and in that silence we meet the Light that lives within us.

The following chapter is a story about a journey into and out of depression, a journey of wounding and healing. It is a good illustration of some of the things I have been discussing.

CHAPTER TWO

Woman Who Walks in Balance

Ancient she was, old and skinny, wrinkled and white haired. She was joyful, and peace flowed around her. We met by chance forty years ago as I traveled through Mexico. We were together long enough for me to listen to her story. Her wisdom transcended the barriers of race, culture, gender, and time itself. I became the younger woman listening respectfully to the voice of the elder. She was the first warrior I ever met. I will always remember her. Her story has danced in my heart these many years. This is the way I remember the telling.

The world I remember is gone. The story that could weave the pieces of that lost world together is also lost, and so I do not remember how the fragments fit together. My people were keepers of the balance. In the living of our lives, we wove the threads of chaos together into harmony. Living and dying, change and movement were woven together in the daily lives of the people and into all of the life that surrounded them. The gift of each life was nurtured. Each life contributed to the whole.

I had seven summers when I was taken from my people. I had already learned to sing in my being with the stone sentinels that guarded our valley. I was learning the language of the "wingeds." I could weave cloth patterns that were tight and straight. My grandmothers were teaching me the art of healing. One day I would be chief as the women in my line had been chief before me.

The strangers came by stealth in the night. They had weapons that could kill at a distance. They killed my mother and my father. They separated the women from the men and the children. They beat the men. They called the women and the children into the center of the village. These strangers told the chiefs that if all of the women did not submit to rape, they would kill all the men and children.

In our world, life is sacred. There were only two laws: honor the woman, for all life comes through the feminine, and do nothing to harm the children. So, the women stepped forward and submitted to the men.

As I watched those men mount the women, I waited for the thunder beings to come and destroy them, but the thunder beings did not come. These men were not human. They had no understanding of what they did. They had no honor. Lovemaking was an act of aggression for them, and I understood as I watched them that these men were less than human because they were born from women they treated as filth. I knew with a cold certainty that this was the end of my people. Nothing would be left.

They killed all the elders and all the children under age five. The rest of us were tied to their horses, taken as slaves to sodomize and rape. They spit on the chiefs and told them they were no longer chiefs; they were cows to be bred for sons. They took us with them from village to village, and we watched the same scene repeated over and over and over.

I do not remember much about when they began to handle me. They called me "whore." I had not yet had my true naming. I was not yet a woman. I had not started on my moon cycles, and I was too young to "cry for a vision." I wondered if "whore" was the only name I would ever know. I felt abandoned by the sacred ones and forgotten. Hate was like a hot knot in my belly. I endured and hoped that I would be able to maim and kill as many of these creatures as possible before I died. Outwardly, I became docile, but inside I waited patiently for the time when I would strike them down. I comforted myself with the songs and stories of my people.

Gradually, the songs and stories began to fade from my mind. I felt numb and dumb. I sank into despair. I was forced to learn to speak to the strangers. I was not allowed to speak to anyone else. If I was not docile and quiet, I was tortured. My body still bears the scars. There was never enough food. They made us fight with each other over the little there was. They wagered on who would win and who would lose. Over time we lost respect for ourselves and for each other. We lost our ability to stay balanced.

I could no longer hear the singing of the stones. I could not understand the language of leaf or bird. I hoped to be blotted out of existence. I began to study these beings who had captured me, so I could kill as many as possible.

When my chance finally came, I killed or wounded more than ten. The others stabbed me in the chest and back and left me in the woods to die.

I woke in a strange place. An old man and an old woman cared for me and nursed me back to health. I begged them to let me die. I tried to explain that I wanted to be blotted out of existence. I tried to tell them I was no longer human. They refused to listen to me, and gradually, my broken body began to mend. I could not sleep without screaming. When I woke I could not control the shaking of my body when I was surprised by a sound. The old man and the old woman held me as I screamed and shook. Gradually, I got better.

One day the old man and old woman said it was time to teach me to become a warrior. It was time to learn to find the balance within myself. They told me that the reason I was numb and dumb was that my spirit had left me while I was being tortured. They promised to teach me to call back my spirit by connecting with energy as it flows in the universe.

Truth can never be lost, only spoken in a different way. I chose to listen to them and trust their teachings. I could always choose to die if what they promised me did not come to pass.

The first part of my training was purification. I worked to remember all that I had heard and seen and felt. I could barely tolerate the hatred I felt for them and for myself. I wanted to rip out my hair and tear off my skin when I remembered. I worked to remember; my only other choice was to die.

Eventually, I learned to put the "rememberings" into images, the images into words, and finally into a story. I learned to step back and watch myself moving in the story. I could not allow my heart to come too close to the story lest I fall backwards into the darkness of those terrible times. I had to learn to hold the story yet stay back and observe. I had to stay far enough back to understand what was happening there without reentering the darkness. Each time I did this, I died a little. As I accepted these little deaths, I began to have an experience of light and life entering my story.

As I went over and over and over the events, the times, the people, and the experiences, I began to encounter glimpses of beauty hidden there. The touch of a friend, the song of a bird, and sunlight on a leaf reminded me that even then not all was dark. I wept because I understood that the sacred ones had not abandoned me. I was just too full of pain to see them. My teachers listened. I began to change in the innermost part of me. The part of me that had been tightly locked up and rigid began to move and change. My body often felt as if it were turning to water. I cried most of the time. My teachers gave me work to do that made me sweat, and over time I began in the telling, and the telling, and the telling of my story, to understand what bound and constricted my heart. My heart began to let go of hate and its bindings.

The process of purification through which these teachers walked with me went on for many, many moons. My story was the sacred circle that held the dark seeds of revenge, hatred, and bitterness, sometimes pierced by the light of beauty and wonder. Slowly, the numbness lifted from my body, and I began again to sense the world around me.

As my awareness flowed, the second part of my training began. I felt the longing of the universe to become. I was so open to life and the feelings of all Creation that I had to learn how to protect myself. I had to learn where I began and where I stopped while yielding to the energy of Creation. This was difficult: relearning to be mentally receptive in my heart and yet holding all my experience in order to understand physically that no matter what I experienced, I could not lose myself.

I had to learn to open and close my being at my own will, not someone else's. I learned to communicate again with the world around me. I learned again to allow the stone people to sing in my bones. I learned again to listen to their whispers as I watched the trembling leaves. The old woman taught me movements for my body that opened me to receive energy in my head, my heart, and in my belly. Gradually, these movements allowed energy to move throughout my body. I do not know how long this took. I only know I learned slowly, and as I learned, I began to feel alive again.

One day the old man told me that I had to learn to speak again with the people who had hurt me. He told me that I would never be free until I had faced them with no fear, no desire, and no despair. He took me to a place called a city, and in that city he taught me to become invisible.

I learned to walk among these people as a child, an elder, a cripple, as a man, and as a woman. I walked among them and learned their ways. I walked among them and saw into their hearts. I walked among them and saw how their spirits had been lost because they believed what people told them rather than what they knew. I learned to sense in my body that I was no longer naked and vulnerable when someone looked at me. These people saw only what I let them see. I could meet someone, and he or she would see me as an old woman. Later that person would see me as a young girl. They saw what I wished them to see. I saw their inner chaos. I began to understand that the balance had been lost for all people, not just my people.

When I returned to my teachers, I brought back the pain of the people I met, and sometimes I felt the invisible world behind Creation groaning and longing for the people to return to themselves.

The old man and the old woman taught me to transform the energies that arose within me when my inner chaos tried to overwhelm me. They taught me about the energy that lives in nature and how that energy could heal me. They taught me how to stand and how to breathe, so I could relax and smile and allow the energy of nature to enter my being. As I learned to relax, the energy of nature taught me to find the places in my body that were constricted with pain. These tight, rigid places vibrated with shame, rage, and fear. Relaxing into these constricted spaces allowed the pain to surface, so I could breathe it out of my body.

I remembered again each event, each wounding, allowing the images to rise to my mind and letting them go gently away from me. As I did this, the stones, the trees, the earth, the water, the sun, the moon, and the creatures of the forest seemed to encourage me to trust what was happening and to keep on. Transformation took place as a gift of nature, a mystery. The gift of transformation would not have been given if I had not done the work. This work took many years, and when it was complete, I was gifted with compassion.

In the end, I was no longer affected by the presence and the emotions of others. My body became healthy, and I became younger and stronger.

The old man and the old woman knew where one of the tyrants who destroyed my people and abused me lived. They told me that if I could encounter this tyrant and remain balanced, I would truly be free from the limitations of my past. They took me to the place where the man lived and worked. I saw him and remembered him. He was the one who killed my mother and my father. He was a wealthy man, the owner of a large factory that wove cloth. I knew I would never truly be free until I faced that tyrant and tested the strength of my learning and healing by remaining in balance.

I was hired because I looked strong. I cleaned up, moved equipment, and kept the workers supplied with material and thread. I began my study of this man. I learned that he employed women and children who worked long hours for little pay. For those he employed, a little was better than nothing. When he spoke, people listened. He liked that. They listened because he had so much money. No one knew or even suspected that he was abusing the women and children who worked for him. The people in the community thought he was a good man who cared for the poor. They did not know there were times when the workers weren't paid. He terrified his workers and ruled them with an iron fist. He was wealthy, respected, and in charge.

When I looked at this man, I was overcome with hatred and overpowered by fear. I felt helpless and slipped back into the pain of wanting to be blotted out of existence. I began with breath and used my breath to relax, moving into the tightness that bound me, and little by little, I let it go. I began to feel lighter and freer.

I noticed the people around me, and I began to help them. I listened. I taught them what I was learning. How to breathe, how to relax, how to let go and keep balanced. The people learned how to protect themselves from the evil this man spewed by breathing and yielding their pain to the Great Source, working to remain in balance.

The people began to trust me because what I was teaching them worked. The tyrant noticed that we remained neutral during his tirades. He saw that we were working to stay in balance, and he became afraid. Since we were no longer responding to his projection of hatred and rage, those emotions returned to him. His fear grew, and he became less and less balanced. Together the people and I began meditating by focusing our attention on our breath, letting go of our pain and taking in the powerful, loving energy of the universe in order to remain focused and balanced. We performed our tasks as perfectly as possible. I waited and trusted that something would happen to set us free.

As the tyrant felt his hatred and rage returning to him, he became more and more violent. He stopped our work and made all of us watch as he abused and molested the children. He taunted us, daring us to stop him. When we did not, he laughed and told us he was a god who could do whatever he wanted, whenever he wanted.

One day something unusual happened. His friends dropped by to take him to lunch for his birthday. At the time he was molesting a little boy, screaming in hatred and rage. This tyrant was finally seen in the light of truth. I don't know how to explain it, but I think this perversion of humanity was exposed for what he was because we clung to the powerful and loving energy of the universe rather than reacting to him. The tyrant was imprisoned, and because he truly believed he was a god, he refused to submit to authority. He fought and cursed the guards who retaliated by letting him sit in his waste and beg for his food. I understood how I was like this man. I too felt hatred and rage. I too wanted to hurt and maim. But I was different from him because I knew I was out of balance, and the wise old woman and the wise old man appeared in my life in response to my longing for healing and wholeness.

I returned to thank the wise old woman and the wise old man, and they gave me a new name. I am called Woman Who Walks in Balance.

The people who listen and hear my story are my people.

My people live.

The story of Woman Who Walks in Balance describes the formation of a drama through a series of terrifying events. Some dramas are more intense than others depending on the level of emotional intensity involved. When we are caught up in a drama, death and transformation are blocked. This story is also a powerful example of death and change, chaos and transformation into a new way of being. All of us experience these cycles, all of us suffer, and all of us must learn to accept, endure, and allow the transformation to take place. First, we must remember who we are.

CHAPTER THREE

Getting to Know Yourself

The following assessment tool will help you learn more about yourself and your drama. When we feel stuck, blocked, misjudged, helpless, victimized, persecuted, or unappreciated, we are caught in some kind of drama. When we have to justify our behavior, when we have to be one up, when we are upset that things did not turn out the way we expected or when we are dependent upon someone or something, we are caught in a drama. When we learn to identify our drama and find out where we are caught, we can let the drama go.

The assessment below should help you identify your drama. Journaling and self-reflection will help you step back from the drama and become aware of how and when it works.

Once you have fleshed out your drama and become familiar with it, you can go on to the next step and begin letting go of it.

Describe Yourself

1. Use four words to describe yourself. I am a person who is:

A.   C.

B.   D.

2. I am a person how has the following strengths and weaknesses:

A. Strengths   B. Weaknesses

    1.   1.

    2.   2.

    3.   3.

    4.   4.

3. The four most important things, events, and/or teachings that people have given me are:

A.   C.

B.   D.

4. Name up to three psychological roles (e.g., scapegoat, peacemaker, listener) that you have played for each of the following people:

A. Mother:

    1.   2.   3.

B. Father:

    1.   2.   3.

C. Siblings:

    1.   2.   3.

5. If I could do anything in the world I want to do, knowing I would not fail, I would:

A.   B.   C.

Describe Your Family

6. Describe your father:

A. List his five most positive qualities: B. List his five most negative qualities:

C. How are you like him?   D. In what ways are you different?

E. Use one word to express how your father described you as a child, an adolescent, and how he describes you as an adult.

  a. Child   b. Adolescent   c. Adult

7. Describe your mother:

A. List her five most positive qualities: B. List her five most negative qualities:

C. In what ways are you like her?   D. In what ways are you different?

E. Use one word to express how she described you as a child, an adolescent, and how she describes you as an adult.

  a. Child   b. Adolescent   c. Adult

8. **Name each of your siblings.**

A.   C.

B.   D.

Name one way you are like sibling: Name one way you are different
                                        from sibling

A.   A.

B.   B.

C.   C.

D.   D.

9. **How did your siblings as a group describe you as a child and as an adolescent, and how do they describe you as an adult?**

a. Child   b. Adolescent   c. Adult

10. **Name four ways you influenced people in your family to get what you wanted.**

A.

B.

C.

D.

11. **Name three ways you were perceived and labeled by your family members that were inaccurate and painful.**

A.   B.   C.

12. Use four adjectives to describe what your life will be like five years from now.

A.   C.

B.   D.

13. In your journal, record any recurring or enduring dreams that you remember from childhood. Note the images in the dream that were most meaningful to you and any impact the dream or the enduring impressions had on you, (e.g., emotional reactions or insights). Summarize your response in as few words as possible.

14. If you could change anything about yourself by wishing, what would it be?

A.   C.

B.   D.

15. How would your friends describe you? Use four adjectives.

A.   C.

B.   D.

16. How would your enemies describe you? Use four adjectives.

A.   C.

B.   D.

17. What four feelings do you never want to feel again?

A.   C.

B.   D.

18. **If you knew you were going to die soon and could so anything that you wanted to do, what would it be?**

19. **Reflect on what it was like for you growing up in your family. What would you:**

A. Feel?   B. Remember?

C. Imagine?   D. Physical experience?

20. **In your journal, name up to four subjects that were hard to discuss in your family.**

21. **Name three things you are most ashamed of regarding your family.**

A.   B.   C.

Name three things you are most proud of regarding your family.

A.   B.   C.

Describe Your Relationships

22. **List three people who have been influential in your development, excluding the family members mentioned above.**

A.   B.   C.

23. **List three positive traits for each person.**

A.   B.   C.

24. List three negative traits for each person.

A.   B.   C.

25. List three positive traits brought out in you by each person.

A.   B.   C.

26. What would you have liked to receive that you were not given by each person?

A.   B.   C.

27. Describe you reaction when the above (#27) happened with each person.

A.   B.   C.

28. List the ways you tried to use your influence to get what you wanted from each person.

A.   B.   C.

29. List your most positive feelings about each person.

A.   B.   C.

30. List your most negative feelings about each person.

A.   B.   C.

31. **How did you react emotionally, physically, and behaviorally when you had negative feelings about each person?**

Emotion

    A.   B.   C.

Physical Sensation

    A.   B.   C.

Behavior

    A.   B.   C.

32. **How did you react emotionally, physically, and behaviorally when you had positive feelings about this person?**

Emotion

    A.   B.   C.

Physical Sensation

    A.   B.   C.

Behavior

    A.   B.   C.

33. **Use your journal to record any ongoing positive and emerging patterns of interaction and communication that appear in your dreams and fantasies about any of your relationships. Record the feelings, memories, physical sensations, behaviors, and images that are meaningful to you about this pattern.**

Feelings:

Memories:

Physical sensations:

Images:

Behaviors:

Meanings:

Our Drama: A Pattern of Reactivity

To complete the following statements, look back to the descriptions you gave of yourself, your family, and your relationships on the previous pages. In the space provided, use two to three words to summarize your answers.

I experience tension or tightness in my body in the following places:

I feel:

I remember:

I react by:

The things that hold the most meaning for me then are:

The images I have are:

My choices are limited by:

The rules and laws I obey are:

The ways I perceive myself are:

The ways I perceive the world around me are:

My center of authority resides in:

What I need most from another human being is:

What I need to do in order to take care of myself is:

What I realize now after doing this assessment is that many of the physical responses, memories, feelings, and behaviors that I have identified in the pages above are ongoing and predictable and part of a negative drama that saps my energy.

Write down your response to this statement.

How can I begin interrupting this negative drama?

Use your journal to draw the images associated with your drama.

How does your energy level change as you interrupt your negative drama?

a. Physically:

b. Mentally:

c. Emotionally:

d. Sexually

e. Spiritually

What behaviors and reactions can you change in order to interfere with your negative drama and the depression it creates? Keep a record of your dreams and experiences of change. It is easy to keep your journal at your bedside and write your dreams down before you get up. Your unconscious will help you by encouraging you, or it may point out your mistakes or reveal your gifts. A chemical change takes place between waking and sleeping, and if you write the dream down before you get up, that may help you remember it. Some people simply do not remember their dreams. If that is the case with you, keep your mind open and receptive to your waking experience, and listen or watch for information that may help you come to grips with the things you need to change and the things you need to face and free yourself from in order to increase your life energy. The following chapter discusses transformation as part of everyday life.

CHAPTER FOUR

Reflection

The assessment in the previous chapter provides you with information about the drama in your life. Take time to read over your responses and find the emotional theme in them. If you can't find the emotional theme, draw a picture of what the theme might be. Put the picture away for a few days, and then look at it again. What does it tell you?

In some ways the theme you are working with is like a depression of your emotions, your body, your mind, your spirituality, or your sexuality. One of these five aspects is out of balance.

Drama is unconscious, which is what makes it repetitive and ongoing. When we are in the grip of a strong emotional theme, our thinking and our ability to observe accurately are not operating. The emotional theme overrides our thoughts and influences the way we relate to ourselves and others. Usually, we are not engaged in drama until something triggers it. For example, we see the movie *Jaws*. A musical theme plays when the shark is sneaking up on someone. That theme is linked with the scary shark. When we hear the theme, we are linked back to our fear of the shark even if we are not viewing the movie at the time.

The story of Woman Who Walks in Balance describes the formation of a drama through a series of terrifying events. Some dramas are more powerful than others, depending on the level of emotional intensity involved. When we are caught up in a drama, death and transformation are blocked.

Each and every one of us has problems that can become dramatic because each of us experiences birth, death, success, loss, joy, sorrow, pain, and suffering. Most of the dramas we experience have an ending. However, some dramas are ongoing. When we find ourselves caught in a similar pattern of feelings, ideas, thoughts, and behaviors, living the same scenario over and over and over, we are caught, handcuffed and shackled, in a sense. The drama is ongoing because we are attached to or dependent upon something within the drama, even though it is depleting our life energy.

When we feel stuck, blocked, misjudged, helpless, victimized, persecuted, or unappreciated we are caught in some kind of drama. When we have to justify our behavior, when we have to be one up, when we are upset that things did not turn out the way we expected, or when we are dependent upon someone or something, we are caught in a drama. When we learn to identify our drama and where we are caught, we can let the drama go.

The assessment in the previous chapter should help you begin to identify your drama. Journaling and self-reflection will also help you step back from the drama and become aware of how and when it works.

Once we have fleshed out our drama and become familiar with it, we can go on to the next step and begin letting it go.

CHAPTER FIVE

Change and Transformation

Long before I became an analyst, change and how change takes place fascinated me. When I was about four years old, my dad decided to raise chickens to make extra money. I asked if I could have one of the cute little chicks for a pet. My dad said it was okay, but the little chick might not like being a pet.

I kept it in a cardboard box with plenty of food and air holes. Despite my care, the chicken died within a day. My dad and I buried it and said some prayers, so it would go to heaven.

The next day I dug up the chick. My father was horrified and asked why I did it. I told him I wanted to see what was going to happen next. My dad assured me that the chick was truly dead, and all that would happen next is that it would slowly turn to dust, and the spirit inside the chicken would go to another dimension called heaven, which is invisible to us. *Turning to dust is something happening,* I thought to myself. *So is going to heaven.* I felt as if I were standing before something very profound, a secret that linked death with change and a great invisible place full of mystery.

I went to college and studied psychology. Psychology is the study of the human body and mind. It is a fledgling science with many books with many words, and yet the truth about psychology is that we know very little about ourselves. One of the things that psychology studies is change: change of behavior, change of mind, change in response to stimuli, change in response to no stimuli, change in relationships, or changes created and experienced by people in general. I learned that change is difficult and that psychopathology is the result of resistance to or the inability to change. I wondered if something in a person's life had to die or be released in order for change to take place.

When we go through change or when we are forced to change by life circumstances, our only choice is how we respond. The first step is to acknowledge and accept the change mentally and emotionally. That acceptance is a "little death." Then we must make a friend of the death that created the change.

How do we make a friend of death? When we truly accept the fact that the loss is real and feel the hurt. As we grieve our loss and accept and turn toward this new life, we begin the process of transformation. The process is invisible, and we are unaware of it. Yet one day we hear a sound or see something that surprises us into a new kind of consciousness, awareness that feels more alive, awake, and aware that wonder and joy are flowing around us.

We experience "little deaths" all the time beginning when we are very young. Look back over your life and remember what it was like to fail at something, to want something and not get it, to lose a friend, to feel misunderstood, to be forced to let go or forced to go in a direction that you did not want to go. These experiences are little deaths that can change and transform us when we accept them. We make a friend of death each time we accept that something has changed or has ended, and we allow ourselves to be transformed. All of Creation participates in this mystery. We alone have a choice to yield to it, so we can be aware we are transforming and cooperate with the process. When we fight this process, we shut down the cycle and become lost and depleted.

CHAPTER SIX

Stories of Depression and Transformation

The following stories present different vantage points into the cycle of change, death, and transformation that lead from depression to light.

The Old Indian Man: One Story of a Journey into Light[2]

Many, many years ago there lived an old Indian man. He grew up on the reservation. When he was six years old, he was taken away from his family and sent to a Christian boarding school where he was forced to speak only English. He was too young to have had training in the traditions and ceremonies of his people that connected them with God, who was called Great Spirit or Sacred Mystery.

When the boy, now a man, returned to his reservation, he married and had children. Like many of the native people, he developed the disease of alcoholism. Somehow he was able to stop drinking, but by that time his wife and children were gone. Life with him was just too hard for them. It took him a long time to create a new life. He remarried, got a job, had more children, and felt as if his life was everything he wanted. However, he began having nightmares and suffered terribly from lack of sleep.

---

2   Sister Jose Hobday told me this story.

No one was able to help him. Finally, in desperation, he visited the old medicine man, one of the leftovers of tribal life that modern society passed by. By then the old man was sixty years of age. The medicine man, who was even older, told him that he was out of alignment with the flow of his own life energy. "I think the Great Spirit is trying to wake you up because you have work to do." Neither of them had any idea what that work was.

The medicine man began to teach the old man the ancient, sacred ways of his people and how they connected with sacred mystery, which is present within all the Creation. Finally, the medicine man told the old man that he was ready to pray for a vision.

The old man went into the sweat lodge to purify himself and then went up into the mountains to pray for a vision. He carried no food or water. There was nothing to distract him. After nine days in the mountains, a hummingbird appeared and told him that he was to teach the ways of his people to the entire world.

The old man came down from the mountain feeling ecstatic, and for the first time in his life he felt a sense of purpose and commitment. He went to the medicine man, told him of his experience, and asked, "What does this mean? How can I do that?"

"The truth of your vision is alive within you," the medicine man replied. "You must allow it to uncover itself over time. I cannot help you. I can only be your friend."

The old Indian man meditated and prayed but found no truth. He studied with the medicine man and learned all he could about his native heritage. For seven years he went up into the mountains to pray. Each time he received the same vision along with a powerful urge to do or to create something.

As the years went on, this urge became increasingly painful for him. He suffered and wept because he could not uncover or understand the truth within him. He felt as if he would walk forever in darkness, but he kept on, year after year, going up into the mountains to pray for a vision.

The old Indian man worked as a handyman. One day he was in the general store buying nails (on the reservation the general store was the only store, and it carried everything). He noticed a man ahead of him buying oil paints and brushes. The old Indian man had never seen them before. He did not know what they were, but something within him recognized them and said, "Yes." Without thinking, he told the cashier that he wanted all the things that the man ahead of him had purchased.

He came home with an easel, canvases, turpentine, brushes, a palette, a palette knife, and oil paints of every color. He set everything up in his home and waited for something to happen, but nothing did. Eventually, he took these things outside and began to paint. He played with the colors and shapes of what he saw behind the reality of everyday life on the reservation. What he saw was beauty, the beauty that glittered behind, above, around, and beneath the joy and pain of his people. He sold his paintings to the manager of the general store, so he could buy more paints.

One day some people came through the reservation on their way to New York. They stopped for supplies at the general store and saw the old man's paintings. They bought them all and hung his paintings in a gallery, and they were purchased almost immediately. Today his paintings hang all over the world as an example of the beauty that lives beneath the spaces and colors of our material word. The old man made the invisible, visible. He went through the process that led him from the death of ignorance into the life and light of fulfillment. It was his everyday journey from depression into life.

We could say this man was very depressed and had to go through a process of healing, which allowed him to do the work that the Creator intended for him to do. He had to die a little to let go of his alcoholism. He died again when he realized he was responsible for losing his family. He erased his history of wrongdoing by asking the Creator for forgiveness and then forgiving himself for what he had done. He felt like a new man. He felt free until he began having nightmares.

His conscious awareness was so far from the message contained in his dream that he experienced it as a nightmare. His nightmare propelled him to ask for help from the medicine man. He received help and was taught to step into silence and "cry for a vision." Even though he received a vision, he had no frame of reference to help him understand how to express it. This entire process of seeking and receiving a vision transformed him, so he could live a life he never could have imagined. When he intuitively recognized the tools he needed to work with and began to paint, his transformation was complete. He was able to fulfill the directive of his vision. He went through powerful changes from death into life.

The Old Monk

Once upon a time, long, long ago, there was a great temple where people went to worship God. Monks and nuns staffed the temple. They lived in constant prayer. They grew their own food and raised and bred their livestock. Their lives were simple; they worked and they prayed.

Somehow the temple became famous, and people visited it from all over the world. The people who came believed that because the monks and nuns were close to God, the visitors could be helped through their prayers.

One of the monks served as the gatekeeper. His job was to control the opening and closing of the gates, teach visitors how to grow closer to God, and pray for their healing.

The gatekeeper began to grow famous, and as he did, he felt increasingly important. He believed he was truly a great monk, special because of the many people who were healed through his prayers and the many more who were helped from his advice. He became so famous that the visitors crowded into the temple, creating disturbances that interfered with the life and prayers of the other monks and nuns. They all left and never returned. There was no one to cook or clean, no one to take care of the animals, and no one to plant the crops and harvest them. The monk survived only because the people who came to visit brought him food.

Finally, the old monk died and went directly to God for judgment. God showed the monk that his life had been filled with ignorance, insensitivity, and self-importance. The monk had hurt many more people than he had healed because he was so full of himself that he could not see the people who needed healing. The monk argued with God and tried to defend his actions, telling God that people *were* healed and made better through him and that he had earned one of the highest places in heaven through his work. God shook her head and said nothing. She understood that the monk could not hear her through the web of lies that he had created about his "being so special." His self-importance and his ignorance had created a great karmic debt, and he would return to life again and again until he was able to face the terrible burden of what he had done to others.

The monk lived thousands of lifetimes. He was always alone. He was never loved, and he never loved anyone. People shunned him. He had to work hard just to sustain himself. He was often tired, hungry, and lonely. He forgot how to pray. He even forgot God.

One day, after finishing his meager supper, he happened to look down at his empty, shiny plate. As he looked at the plate, he saw and felt an image of such beauty and perfection that he was stunned beyond words, beyond thought. He felt held by this presence and begged the presence to hold him close and never, ever leave him.

Gradually, the presence faded, and as it did, the monk felt as if he had died. He sobbed because he felt incomplete and lost, abandoned and terribly alone. As he came to face and accept the truth of his aloneness, he was inundated with memories of his past lives. These memories haunted him while awake and asleep. He experienced the suffering of all of the people he had touched with his ignorance and self-importance. He finally remembered arguing with God and felt ashamed and begged for forgiveness.

Seasons passed, and so did years. He did not get sick or age. He felt as if he were being transformed but did not know how or why.

Then one day God spoke to him. "It is time for you to leave this place and serve me," she said.

The old monk, transformed now, left his hut and followed wherever God led him. He did whatever God told him. He counseled beggars, and he counseled kings. He blessed the lonely, the outcasts, and the beautiful. He spoke to all he met about the presence of God within each and every one of us. His name was Lao Tzu.

The cycles of death and transformation are much clearer in the story of the old monk. Until he was able to let his ignorance and self-importance die, he could not accept the transformation that awaited him.

Not only did the old monk have a destiny, he was reborn again and again until he fulfilled that destiny. It is the same for each of us.

It doesn't matter how long it takes or how many times we choose to avoid it; we will eventually complete the destiny we are given and fulfill the purpose for which we were made. When we are learning to fulfill our destiny, we are journeying from the ignorance of death and transformation into the fullness of life. It is a quiet and simple journey hidden from others and often from ourselves. This movement from death and transformation into life is a process that increases our life energy as we move in harmony with the cycles of nature and chance.

As we move through life making our choices, we increase or decrease our life energy, hopefully becoming more aligned with the universe and nature, more vibrant, more conscious, and more alive. The Chinese call our life energy "chi," which I discuss in the following chapter.

CHAPTER SEVEN

Chi

Chi is an invisible energy that flows throughout the body following the flow of the blood. The ancient seers could perceive this energy in human beings as well as in all of nature. The stronger the chi, the greater the health, the longer the life, and for human beings, the greater their wisdom. The Chinese science of medicine is built upon the idea of monitoring the flow of chi. Symptoms and disease are caused by the blockage of chi, diverted from its normal flow. Treatment using acupuncture and herbs gradually restores the normal circulation of chi. Diet, exercise, breathing techniques, and meditation are considered necessary for increasing the level of chi for health and spiritual development. When our chi is blocked, we have symptoms, one of which is depression. Our chi can be blocked emotionally, physically, mentally, spiritually, and/ or sexually.

Chi is invisible, but we can feel it. We describe ourselves as having "low energy" or "lots of energy," feeling "up" or feeling "down." This book is about raising our levels of chi: emotionally, physically, mentally, spiritually, and sexually. When our chi levels are high in all five aspects, we are healthy.

The practice of medicine in our culture is based upon observing the symptoms of disease and treating those symptoms. The idea of chi is not a part of our western medical practice. Depression is treated with medication, therapy, diet, and exercise. These treatments focus on the body and on the mind. The idea of increasing one's life energy physically, emotionally, mentally, sexually, and spiritually is rarely included in the treatment. Yet in order to face and let go of the drama associated with the depression, you must learn to raise your energy—your chi. When you are working on increasing your life energy, you are placing yourself in charge of your life rather than allowing depression to be in charge.

CHAPTER EIGHT

Grandma and the Tyrants

My ninety-two-year old grandmother broke her hip and was hospitalized. She was scheduled for surgery the following day at 9:00 a.m. I went to the hospital to wait until the surgery was over. I waited for six hours and heard nothing. I got concerned and paged her surgeon to see if something was wrong. The surgeon told me that she had not been operated on because the anesthesiologist was unwilling to anesthetize her due to my grandmother's heart problems.

I understood why the anesthesiologist was afraid. (If an anesthesiologist has a certain number of deaths during or right after surgery, he or she is suspected of error and is closely examined.) I also understood that my grandmother would die a horrible and long -drawn-out death if she did not have the surgery.

I asked to speak with the anesthesiologist and confronted him with my concerns. He didn't say a word, but from the way he tensed his body and thinned his lips, I could tell he would not operate on my grandmother. Then I told him that if it looked like Grandma was going to die, he could wheel her into the recovery room and let her die there, so his record would not be damaged. If he refused to allow the operation to take place, I would sue him for malpractice.

Grandma had the surgery and made a great recovery. I was sickened by what happened and wondered how many other grandmas didn't get the surgery they needed because they had no one to advocate for them. The man was a tyrant. A tyrant is someone who feels entitled to take by rape, robbery, intimidation, murder, abuse, or taxation. Most tyrants operate through ignorance. All tyrants lower our energy, and all tyrants are a part of the drama. The anesthesiologist did not intend to be a tyrant; he was protecting himself. Such tyrants are all around us, but most of us don't believe they exist and don't want to hear about them, unless on the news.

Several years later, Grandma died. She was in the hospital portion of her retirement home. She asked her nurse to call me and tell me to come and see her. When I arrived, Grandma told me that she died and went out of her body to a place where she had to cross a wide river. An angel told her that she was not ready to cross the river yet and to return to her body until it was time for her to cross. Grandma cried when she told me this because she wanted to cross the river and go home to God.

Two days after we spoke, Grandma had a massive stroke. My family and I visited her once a week and pushed her around in a wheelchair. She did not recognize us, but she was always happy to see us. Grandma had a hard life. She was born out of wedlock. Her mother washed clothes to earn a living. When Grandma was four years old, her mother met and married a farmer. They had four more children. Grandma was the oldest of five. Her brothers and sisters taunted her and called her the "bastard." She loved school but had to leave school at the age of ten and keep the records for her mother's laundry business. When she grew up, she married and had two sons, one of whom was my father. Her husband disappeared when the boys were very young, and when she was not working as a laundress, the three of them visited morgues hoping to find and identify their husband and father.

Grandma never had much money and worked hard at whatever jobs she could find. She rarely smiled or laughed. I think she was depressed for most of her life and dealt with it by working from dawn to dusk.

After her stroke, she was changed. She became like a child—delighted with everyone and everything. It was as if her painful personal history had been erased, and she was free from the awful memories and the burdens that life had forced her to carry. Instead, she was experiencing life through the eyes of a delighted child. When she finally died, her burdens had become so light that she could cross the river.

She was a member of her church for over fifty years, and her minister talked with me about doing a memorial service for her. I told him the story that Grandma told me about the river and asked him to include it in her memorial service. He said he couldn't talk about something like that because it might interfere with people's religious beliefs. I thought about the minister and the anesthesiologist and concluded that each man was more interested in covering his ass than dealing with truth. Later it occurred to me that what these men were really afraid of on some level was the cycle of death itself and the transformation associated with it. They were ignorant, and their ignorance made them fearful of what they did not know or understand.

CHAPTER NINE

Tyrants and Treasures

We need a high level of energy to stay healthy and happy. Over time I have noticed that when I am most vulnerable, people enter my life and begin taking bites out of me. This phenomenon is not unique to me. I believe that tyrants come into our lives to victimize us and lower our energy mentally, physically, emotionally, spiritually, and/or sexually. We can decide how we respond to tyrants. We can give in, become a victim, and wallow in the pain, or we can leave the tyrant, reflect on our experience, and learn from it in order to increase our energy. This is a difficult concept to accept, and yet the roles in each drama are the victim, the rescuer, and the tyrant.

I was raised as a Catholic. One of the things I was told is that the devil travels the world seeking the ruin of souls. I believed what I was told. The way I thought about it then was in terms of war, famine, and human suffering in general. As I matured, I learned that nothing in this world is black and white or clearly good or evil. It finally occurred to me that evil works energetically, subtracting strength from us mentally, physically, emotionally, spiritually, and/or sexually.

Vulnerability and helplessness attract tyrants, and tyranny is alive and well all around us. Most tyrants become that way because they have been tyrannized. Others become tyrants because they are greedy, lustful, angry, or frightened. The rest become tyrants because they enjoy inflicting pain.

The effect of being tyrannized is the loss of energy, and when energy is lowered, we become shut away from the beauty of life. The Light around us is always there, but as we move into depression, we lose parts of our ability to perceive the Light.

When we are depressed, we can be certain one or more tyrants is at work in our life. Tyrants operate by putting us down, using us, limiting our choices, placing us in a category, cheating us, or doing whatever they can to let us know they are better, smarter, or stronger than we are. They even come to our door or call us on the telephone us to sell us a product that we don't want or need. They feel entitled to tell us what to do or how we can improve. Tyrants are alive and well, and they lower our energy.

One day I pulled into the parking lot at the liquor store to buy wine. It happened to be a double-wide space, so people could pull in and out. Two other double-wide spaces were available for people to use. I got out of the car to get my purse out of the trunk when a man who was parked next to me started yelling at me. "Can't you see that you pulled into a double-wide spot?" he asked. "What's wrong with you?" The man was somewhere in his late fifties. I was in my late seventies.

I looked at the man, then picked up my purse, and walked into the store. He followed me, yelling that I didn't care what I did and that I was an irresponsible person who was going to cause an accident. He really worked hard to get me to react. He finally backed off when people started coming out of the store.

The incident reminded me of being seven years old on the playground at recess.

Penny candy was readily available on the way to school, and I bought wax teeth to wear and play with. An older, bigger boy came up to me, punched me in the wax teeth, and broke them. My mouth was a little sore.

He joined a group of boys, and I went over to him holding my broken wax teeth and asked him why he broke them. His friends had not seen him hit me. They looked at him and said, "What's wrong with you?" I walked away, but the incident troubled me because I knew the boy who hit me was jealous of my penny candy and felt entitled to hit me. It was not until his friends confronted him that he felt shame, not for what he had done but for getting caught.

When some of the Native American tribes fought, they did not kill, they "counted coup." They touched their enemy with a thick stick, and when the enemy was touched, he had to turn around and leave the fight. I "counted coup" on the boy because he didn't want his friends to know he was a bully. I exposed him to his friends and made it clear to them that he was a bully and that if he hurt me again, I could go to one of his friends for help. He had to let go of the fight.

When we encounter tyrants, we are encountering a teacher. We have no control over how or when a tyrant enters our life. They come to pull us down and to lower our energy. The only choice we have is to find a way to keep increasing our energy levels using the tools we are given. The final tool is forgiveness. Sometimes I have said to myself, *So, I got stomped on, and now I have to forgive* _____. Yes, we do. It is a spiritual "law." We are forgiven for our sins at the level we forgive those who have sinned against us. Tyrants do real damage to our soul, and our soul records the experience. The big secret is that when we think of them, we can choose to pray for them, and when we pray for them, we erase their recording from our soul, and that sets us free. We earn strength and freedom. That is the treasure the tyrant brings us: strength and freedom.

Spiritual Tyrants

I was a devout Catholic, but I left the Church in 1983. As an analyst, my first patient was a nun who was an assistant pastor at a nearby parish. Three families had come to her separately to tell her that one of the priests was sexually abusing their sons. We discussed the situation, and she decided to have the families meet as a group. They met several times and finally decided to set up an appointment with the cardinal. He told that that if they decided to make the abuse public, he would take them to court and have their sons testify in great detail about what they had experienced. (When a person has experienced trauma and speaks about it, the person relives the trauma.) The families told the cardinal that they would make the matter public anyway. (The offending priest had faced no consequences and had simply been transferred to another parish.) In response, the cardinal gave them a great deal of money to remain silent. After that, I could no longer attend or support the Church in any way. I knew that if the cardinal knew, Rome knew, and since there were no consequences, the abuse was being covered up from the top. This matter was finally made public thirty years later in a documentary done by Front Line called *Secrets of the Vatican.*

After I had my fifth child, I had an operation that prevented any more pregnancies. I went to confession and told the priest that I had the operation because I did not think I could parent any more children. At that time the Church taught that birth control was sinful. I asked the priest if my conscience had overridden the Church's teaching. He told me that it had. "Please don't tell anyone I told you that," he said. I was stunned. What was he afraid of?

One of the most damaging things done to Catholics was the teaching that sexual intercourse could only be performed with the intention of conceiving a child. What were those men thinking when they inserted themselves into sexual relations between a man and a woman? This teaching created terrible problems in poor Catholic countries. I saw the results in Mexico. Women kept bearing children because the priests told them they could not practice birth control. They had too many children to care for. Eventually, the mothers abandoned them, and these children grew up with only each other to cling to. They had no limits, no rules of conduct, no authority over them to teach them morality. They only had each other. They ran in gangs. I saw them in Mexico City and Oaxaca. They learned to cheat, lie, steal, and use their combined power to get whatever they wanted. Many of them rose to fill the ranks of the cartels involved in drugs and prostitution. Years later I saw a quote by Pope Francis saying to the poor of South America, "Stop breeding like bunnies." Later this same pope blamed capitalism and the United States for creating the poverty in developing countries, but he never addressed the issue of how overpopulation contributes to poverty.

History is filled with tyrants, and history is written by those tyrants who win and use history to cover their mistakes. Tyrants are real, and the first step in dealing with them is to accept the fact that they exist. The second step is to expect to be tyrannized but to do what you can to avoid them.

When we accept the fact that tyrants exist, we can be prepared to deal with them. Remember: every drama contains the victim, the tyrant, and the savior.

The Most Difficult Tyrant

The tyrant that has been hardest for me to deal with was my first Jungian analyst. To be accepted as a candidate at the Jung Institute in Chicago, a person had to be in a training analysis for two years with a member of the Chicago Society of Jungian Analysts. When I called the institute to ask about the requirements for training, the man I spoke with was the director of training at the time. He seemed nice, and I did not know any analysts, so I asked him if I could see him for analysis.

I began meeting with him in the fall of 1981. His first statement to me was, "I absolutely fell in love with you when I read your history. Your request for entry into the program was touching." (Before applying to become a Jungian analyst, I had worked as a therapist for ten years.) Two years later, I was accepted into the training program, and then my troubles really began.

I saw this man once a week for over four years. In the fourth year, I began to feel increasingly uncomfortable with him and told him so. I asked him to speak with one of his colleagues about our relationship because I felt there was something terribly wrong between us. After I said that, he stood up and started yelling at me. "I am a master, a master analyst, and you are a nothing. Get out of my office now!" He herded me out of his office. He was so angry that I felt physically threatened.

It was traditional to have a male and a female analyst during training. Shortly after I was accepted into the training program, I started analyzing with Mary Loomis. She was the only other analyst with several children. She was from Detroit, and I began seeing her there. I would fly there on a Friday evening and see her Friday evening and Saturday morning and then fly home.

As soon as I got home from the male analyst's office, I called Mary and told what had happened. She told me not to speak of it to anyone. A previous candidate, a woman, had been sexually involved with her supervisor. She felt taken advantage of and reported it to the training committee (those analysts who oversaw the training program). The male analyst involved received a slap on the wrist, and she was victimized for the rest of her time in training. Mary was one of the few analysts who helped her.

One of the requirements of training was that candidates be evaluated three times a year by a committee of senior analysts. I was told that I had to make extensive changes in order to progress in my training, though I was not told what I had to change. I was totally in the dark and stuck. I was required to attend classes and remain in analysis and supervision, but I was not allowed to take the first set of examinations. My classmates passed me by. I completed my training ten years after I was thrown out of the analyst's office. It was very expensive, and I really struggled with depression as a result. Later I learned that this man had discussed me with members of my committee and told them I was neurotic.

Several years later that same analyst presented at an international conference in Paris. (I was still a candidate in training at that time.) The topic of his lecture was "Countertransference Issues with a Borderline Patient," and I was the patient in question. A borderline patient is a person who is in and out of psychosis and cannot remain in a relationship because the he or she is unable to be securely connected to anyone. (By then I had been married for twenty-three years and was raising five children with my husband.) The analyst was one of the keynote speakers, and everyone who attended the conference was able to attend his lecture. He presented my dreams, my struggles, and my life's journey to over a thousand people.

The analyst chose an international conference to get the attention he seemed to need.[3] My classmates, who attended the conference returned home and told me that he had presented a case and they recognized he was talking about me. I felt as if I had been raped. I completed the training without saying a word about him. My silence and containment during training protected me.

It is terribly painful to be betrayed by a person you love and respect, and yet, unless you forgive and let it go, you will suffer from depression.

The "Levitated" Few

Problems occur in relationships when *taking* is the primary mode of relating rather than *cooperating*. When taking is the norm, a "one up/one down" form of communication develops. How does this happen? I call it the "levitated" syndrome.

In my lifetime I have joined or become a part of different groups, and the "levitated few" have been present in every one of them. People who "levitate" have not studied or questioned or thought about things. They have not earned knowledge. Instead they raise themselves up and claim mastery over the conversation, spouting opinions and silencing dialogue.

---

3   What transpires between a client and a therapist is confidential. State laws protect patient confidentiality, and if confidentiality is breached, the therapist can lose his or her license. I did not report the analyst to the state licensing board. I did not wish to be a part of more drama.

I have met many of the "levitated few" in my life and learned to avoid them. If I could not avoid them, I learned to ignore them. They are fairly benign tyrants, unless their "level of levitation" is challenged.

Stalking Death

The most horrifying tyrant is an entity called "stalking death," as named by some native American tribes. This entity shows up at horrifying deaths. It feeds on energy produced by terrible suffering and is a prime mover in creating that suffering. When we read or hear about a death or deaths that are horrifying and feel the cold breath of hatred and despair, we are encountering "stalking death." It is said that "stalking death" takes everything from us—past lives, future lives, and what we have earned in this lifetime. It cannot take the spirit itself. Victims attract this predator when hope, joy, and love are gone.

Years ago I knew a married couple, Bob and his wife, Margaret. They were colleagues and friends. He was a very successful analyst and author. She was an analyst and teacher. I traveled to South America with her, and we had a wonderful time.

Life events separated us, and I lost touch with them. One night I Googled them to find their address and phone number, so I could reconnect with them. I found them and was confronted with the fact that Bob had killed Margaret and then himself. I spoke with people who knew them to try to understand what had happened. I learned that Bob had developed a form of dementia. He was not aware of any cognitive changes and became grandiose and paranoid, believing he was enlightened while perceiving the people around him as attacking him. He made poor investments and lost all their money. As far as I know, Margaret did not ask anyone for help or talk about the problems they were having. They were forced to sell their beautiful home because of the debt they accumulated. Following the sale, the realtor tried to get into the home to make sure it was ready for the new owners, but she was locked out. Finally, she called the fire department. They broke into the house and found the couple dead inside. Stalking death leaves no treasures behind; only pain. How I wish I had contacted Margaret earlier. How I miss her.

When we are confronted with the heinous and the horrible, the unimaginable, we cry out, "Oh God." Even those who do not believe cry out a "Goddamn" once in awhile. This is not an accident or a bad habit. This is how we are made. We can deny it, forget it, or fight it. It is still the way we are made. The following chapter presents what I trust is God's response to us.

CHAPTER TEN

The Song of the Creator

Before the universe began, the Creator
was and is, always and forever.
In the beginning of Creation, the Creator SANG.

As the song emerged, the heavens and the earth came
into being.
Each and every note of the Creator's song became an entity
unto itself,
round and perfectly pitched.
The Creator's breath permeated all.
Each and every part of Creation began through the
Creator's breath.
As breath was drawn in, that breath became the feminine,
the receptive principle of life.
As breath was expelled, that breath became the masculine,
the active principle of life.
The feminine and masculine perceived one another, and as they
did, they felt such great love for each other that they
came together
and merged as the Creator inhaled.

As the Creator exhaled, they separated in order to observe
each other, and as they did, their love deepened.

The universe began, and all that was created inhaled
and exhaled
in harmony with the Creator.
The Creator's breath has no limits and no dimensions.
The breath of Creation has limits, and these limits
brought forth time.

Time flowed over eons like water flowing over stones.
As it flowed, the breath of the human creation was distanced
From the breath of the Creator.

Distance from the Creator's breath caused Creation
to become unbalanced.
Breath changed, becoming too short or too long, too stilted
or too expansive, too little or too much, too ragged or
too smooth.

This imbalance produced anger and rage, fear and terror,
pride and lust,
shame and desire, bitterness and despair

As these things came into being, they possessed the minds,
the bodies,
the spirits, and the souls of the human creation.
The direct perception of the Creator's presence within each
and every one of us was lost.
Creation began to plunder and destroy itself, destroying its
own nature.

God's heart was troubled, and the Creator grieved because
humans were becoming crippled and bent, and thus did
God speak to her creation.
I place my words into your being, and as they move through you
like water poured out from a cup, they quench the thirst
of my creation.

Let go of worry and self-importance.
Your self is important to me.
Listen to me with your heart.

Sink into your body, and find my silence within you.
Yield to me those things that arise within you to block
that silence.
Yield your fear.
In my eyes you are pure.

I desire to hold you close to me, so you
will remain pure.
Sink into that silence where I reside within you, and I will
renew and refresh you.

I have chosen you from the beginning of time.
Yield all that you are to me.
I will not absorb you.
That is the mistake fear makes.
I do not absorb; I enlighten.
I fill you with light.
Yield all that you are to me, and be filled with me
as you yield.

My creation is one.
My delight is that you are part of my creation as I am,
yet separate from all things, as I am.
I have chosen you to share in my very essence.
I have called to you across many lifetimes.

For thousands of lifetimes you have gone out from me
as I exhale, and for thousands of lifetimes you have
returned to me with my breath.
I am your fulfillment and your completion.

I am your deepest beauty.
I am the ground of all that you experience.

Yield your every breath to me.
Follow your breath, and behold me breathing you into
being.
Behold me breathing you into time.
I call you forth through breath and time.
Receive me.

Expel the darkness within you as you breathe out.
Stand before me, naked and transparent.
I see all that you are.
I love you with a love that can never die.
What you love, I love.
What you see, I see.
What you hear, I hear.
I am the strength that sustains you.

I am reshaping and refining what you know and
what you believe.
I am reshaping and refining earth as you know it.
I am reshaping souls.
I am forgiving and reshaping what you call karma.

Turn toward me, and choose me.
This choice will be made clear within each
human heart, and each human
heart will choose.

Sin affects your senses and your mind, creating
rigidity and distortion.
Sin brings forth suffering.
Sin causes your spirit to move away from me.
The decline of the human spirit has caused me

anguish, for I made you to be my
closest companions.

To restore your body, mind, soul,
and spirit, this is what you
must do.
Let go of attachments.
Let go of dependency.
Let go of hatred and jealousy and war.
Yield all that you are, all that you have been, and
all that you will be to me.

I will re-create you.
The process will be painful.
Do not be afraid, for I will ease your pain.
This process will be silent.
It will not be visible to you or to others.
Trust me.
Allow me to work in the deepest aspects of
your being and endure.

Follow my voice as you do when you listen
to wind moving through leaves. I speak in
your deepest heart.
Follow my heart as the sun follows the horizon.

The very stones of the ground feel my despair,
my grief over my crippled and bent creation.
I can no longer let go of what brings pain to
the innocent.
I will discipline those who rape the innocent.
They will be lost and unmade.
Yet nothing I have made is wasted.
Think on this.

This is my intent for you.
I wish you to be still.
Listen.
I will show you how to bring yourself
into balance.
Breathe in, and I send my very breath
into your being.
Breathe out, and in your breathing out, let go of
what is not, what is not you,
what is not me.
The truth is simple.
With every breath, you become I.
With every breath, I become you.
This is my will.
My pleasure.
My joy.
Together we are beauty.

There is to be nothing between thee
and me; no book, no temple, no priest,
and no ritual.
Hold to me.
I am your only hope, your only love.

I knit you together in your mother's womb.
Knit you together with my love, my presence.
Naked were you born, and naked will you die.
I am with you before birth.
I am with you after death.
I am the deepest Truth of all that you know,
all that you have experienced, and
all that you have seen.
In that small space between life and death, I am
with you always.

Did you know that when you sleep you
rest in me?
I speak to you, and you remember my words
in your dreams.
My words bubble up from the center of your body,
become present to you when your
mind is quiet.

You have been taught to believe that to be human
means your very nature is dirty,
ugly, and sinful.
You have been taught that in order
to approach me, you must discipline your evil
nature and free yourself from sin.
That is the great lie.
I am within you and all around you.
Graciously accept this truth, and allow yourself to
come into my presence.

There are those who wish to gain power
rather than walk in my presence.
Those who seek that power stand
between my creation and me.
Do you perceive the damaged earth,
the polluted water, and the
dirty air that has arisen
from the taint of human greed
and desire?

I have called many into my presence.
Few have responded.
Those who do not respond suffer
because I am absent from them.

Human suffering came into being
when brother killed brother.
This event pierced the veil of protection
that I made to surround the earth.
Energetic beings that you call angels
entered your dimension.
Some of these have chosen to go their
own way instead of following
my way.

They envy my love for you and make
every effort to tear you down, so
they can feast on your life energy.
When I am present, I lift the veil
that covers your ignorance.
I protect you.
I teach you.
I give you my wisdom,
my knowledge,
my peace, and
my contentment.
You do not need much to live.
Yet to survive you must live in me.

Do not create fantasies about
what has happened in
the past or what will
come in the future.
Allow your awareness to remain in the NOW.
It is only in the NOW that I am present to you.

When you indulge in fantasy, you remove yourself
from my presence.
There is a difference between fantasy
and preparation.

You prepare for change.
You indulge in fantasy.
Meditate on this, and you will understand
the difference between preparation
and fantasy.
Let go of concern about what people
may think of you
or what they may say about you.

Karma creates the way you
perceive reality, and from karma comes fear.
Fear of death creates the fantasy of
annihilation.
You cannot be annihilated.
Suffering is born from the fantasy of
annihilation.

False perceptions are born from fantasy.
The patterns of thought and action that emerge
from false perceptions cover truth.
When truth is hidden, these patterns endlessly
repeat themselves and interfere with respect
and peace and gradually interfere
with my will and my way.
Be rigorous in letting go of fantasy.
Discipline yourself to uncover the illusions
that make truth unrecognizable.
When truth is lost to you,
I am lost to you because
you are unable to perceive me.

The discipline of silence requires that you
listen instead of reacting.
Reacting limits your freedom.

Reacting constricts your ability to perceive,
your ability to KNOW.

You have been taught, and you believe that
relationships with other humans
are necessary for your health
and your survival.
That is a lie.
Unless a relationship is grounded in me,
the relationship will fail.
All things come from me and return to me.
No relationship can endure without me.
No person and no thing can fulfill your
needs or meet your expectations.
All that IS comes from me, through me, and
with me.

Where I am not present, relationship is
only a fantasy.
Think on this, and understand that suffering
is born from fantasy.

One of the first lies you were told is that
you are misshapen and ugly.
The second lie is that another person or another
thing can lift you out of that
misshapen ugliness.

Be still and think on these things.
Observe how these lies have shaped the way
you live and will shape the way
you die.

Observe how these lies have caused the
suffering that comes from desire

and the need to accumulate.
Let go of fear, and let go of worry.
Release them.
It is these things that hide me from your
perceptions.
You have been trained to fear since
childhood.
Ask me and I will show you how to
let go of that fear.
I cannot help you unless you ask.
Do not ask just for yourself; ask
for all my creation because you
are a part of it, and it is a part
of you, just as I am.

Let go of your attachment to the internal dialogue
that continually troubles your mind.
When you become aware of the ongoing internal
conversation, give it to me, and allow me
to fill the emptiness left in your mind
with my presence and my love.

When you are truly alive, you will be grateful
for life, you will love and create,
and you will be curious and filled
with wonder and delight.
These are the gifts I have given you.
To use them correctly, you must be
grounded in my presence
and my love.

When we are truly together,
you need not fear devils.
Tell them to go away.
They have no power over you.

Their power comes from the fear that
creates lies.

Be in me as I am in you.
I will not enter your mind uninvited.
That would be an abomination.

I wish to share with you, to create a dialogue
between us.
My delight is a conversation between us.
When you forget me, when you turn away
from me, I suffer.
Does it amaze you that I love you
that much?

I will not prevent the damage that evil creates. I must
allow it, for it is a part of my way beyond your understanding.
Yet as you cling to me, I radiate through you, and
through you I bring light to my creation.
Cling to me with your every breath, and my
mercy will pour through you to
my creation.

There are those around you who wish to
cause you grief and pain.
They wish to destroy my knowledge and
my understanding at any cost.
As your perception moves closer to truth, you will
become more vulnerable, and many will
choose to hurt you.
Perceive them, avoid them, and
do not engage them in any way.
You cannot help them.
Keep your attention focused on my presence within you.
I will deal with your enemies.

You have been taught that in order to be humble
you must demean yourself before others.
That is a waste of your time.
To be humble is to know you need me.

You have sought teachers, and you
have not been taught.
I am your teacher.
You can learn from no other.
Think on these things.
There is beauty in death.
There is beauty in birth,
in stillness,
in motion.
Choose to perceive my beauty.

Do not be afraid when you see the hatred
within the many.
Do not be offended by their violence.
Lift and yield all that you perceive to me.
As you do, I will send my angels to help them.
As you perceive each one, yield each one to me.
I will receive each one and bring them hope.

My mercy and my justice are feminine.
Many have persecuted and repressed the
Feminine, and in so doing they have
hardened my justice and repressed
my mercy.
You can no longer allow anyone to tear
you down or take from you
and not give back.
Let go of them.
Set yourself free from those who feel entitled
to take your energy and use it

as if it belongs to them.
Choose to be alone rather than be used and depleted.
Understand and perceive this terrible truth.

I have set you free, and never again will you be
alone, for I am always with you.
No one and nothing has power over you
unless you give it.

Reflect upon your life, and let go of
those events that trouble you.
Embrace what you have suffered,
learn from it, and then let it go.

Let what you receive come through you
to me.
This is hard for you but not impossible.
Pride interferes with your focus.
You say to yourself, "I am doing this.
I am doing that.
I am doing well.
I am not doing well."
When you find pride blooming within you
shift your focus to Me
over and over and over,
time after time after time.

Your pride will be winnowed into
small pieces.
These small seeds will nourish
your spirit because you are
turning to me rather than turning
toward the promise of
empty success.

Sin is that which degrades and
dishonors my presence
within you,
nothing more and nothing less.
Only I can free you from sin.
No church, no religious belief system, and
no human being can free you from sin.

Know that we are merged and yet separate.
Separation from me creates yearning.
Separation from me creates wisdom.
I created you to know and to understand
your experience, so we can share
what you have learned.

My will shapes all things.
I allow evil.
I allow sin.
These things also shape
your experience.

Do not make the mistake of believing
you are secure.
Let go of your fear of change.
Each letting go is a "little death."
Let go of your fear of death.
Do not fear the transformation
all deaths bring.

I am there in the air you breathe,
in the waters you drink.
Allow yourself to become aware
of this truth.
I am present in the deepest center
of your being, and

I choose to be,
from moment to moment
to moment.
Accept yourself as I have made you.
That is all.

When you sin it becomes a habit
that covers your awareness.
More sin creates more covering.
When your awareness is covered,
you have shut yourself away
from my will, my presence,
and my love.
You become a two-dimensional being
who is numb and dumb and blind,
a caricature of what I have made you.
Then you lie to yourself and blame
your suffering on external events.

Loneliness terrifies you;
let it go.
Fear of death terrifies you;
let it go.
Relax into terror when you
feel it.
Allow yourself to truly feel it,
then yield it to me
It is through your yielding,
your allowing me to enter
you more deeply, that you
become the truth that I have
made you to be.

Let go and turn to me.
Let go and allow yourself to fall

into my deep, wide heart.
Seek my presence within you, for
this is the only way I can
sustain you.

Let go of the ways you order your
perceptions, and yield your
perceptions to me.
"How?" you ask.
This is the way:
turn to me, and allow me to erase
what does not belong, what chains
you, the lies that lead you to despair,
the lies that lead to rage.
Turn to me, and I will do the rest

You do not have the right to do damage
to yourself or to others.
You simply do not have the right.
Cherish your life,
cherish your being,
and cherish others.
It is I who gives life.
It is you who must cherish life.
Forgive all who have hurt you.
Each of you is an individual, unlike
any other.
Do not compare with one another
because it is impossible to do so.
Those who describe levels of
spirituality, levels of connection
to Me are liars and frauds.
There are no levels, only the fulfillment
of each one of you in me.

When people speak to you of levels,
ignore them, for they are fools.

Do not concentrate on levels;
concentrate on me.
My wisdom does not come from
the world around you, and
sometimes it is so foreign to
what you know that you can
be frightened and surprised
by it.
Cling to me, and allow my
wisdom to transform you.

I want you to sing on one
note, with one word,
ah, ah, ah, ah.
Smile as you sing.
Your mind cannot call me;
only your heart can call me.
That is why I want you to sing
in the voice of a stuttering child.
It will remind you of your purity.
You are pure in my eyes.
I see you as whole and complete,
pure and noble and kind.
When you sing to me this way,
you are releasing your sin to me,
so I can lift it from you and
be more fully present within you.
When I am present, I heal your heart
from those people, those things
that stand between thee and me.

Every person has a gift.
Each gift is unique and is the
manifestation of the way
you serve me.
Your gift is embedded in what you
need and what you desire.
The gift is not yours; it is mine.
I breathe this gift through you when
you seek me, when you allow me,
and many are blessed through
this gift.
You do not need to know the gift or
control it.

My love moves through you to
release the dark spirits held
in this dimension.
When a troubled soul is set free,
you work my will by
exuding my presence.

During difficult times you must turn
your attention away from your
thoughts and your fears and
concentrate on your heart
center where I reside.
Imagine this center opening
and closing.
As you open, breathe me in,
and as you close, breathe
me out.
Be steadfast in this practice, and
do not allow your intent to waver.

This is hard work for you but
not impossible.
Those who read these words are blessed.
Those who choose to
trust me are truly free.
Those who read these
words and do what is asked
will be filled with joy and
know the peace of my presence.

The message of this long poem speaks of how much we are cherished and loved by the One who made us. Even though my friends died a terrible death, I trust they will be reshaped and healed. When we pray and when we yield our being to God, we are truly on that journey from depression into light.

CHAPTER ELEVEN

Death, Depression, and Transformation

In 1969 my friend Doctor Elisabeth Kubler Ross wrote the book, *On Death and Dying*. Her colleagues at the University of Chicago vilified her for discussing patients who were dying at a hospital that wanted publicity for people getting well. At that time death was not discussed with patients. It was like an enormous elephant in the room, carefully avoided and never noticed. It was whispered about but never discussed.

This attitude troubled Elisabeth, a psychiatrist on the hospital staff. She decided to ask patients who were diagnosed with a terminal illness about their experience. She began her interviews with patients she found on the wards who wanted to talk about their experience, and with the help of a minister, she began taping the conversations.

Somehow the mainstream media heard about the interviews and became interested. This was something that had never been done before. They wrote about her work, and her picture was on the cover of *Life* magazine. Many of the doctors criticized her publicly and viciously, but Elisabeth kept going. Based on this research, she wrote her first book, *On Death and Dying*, which is still used today in schools that train medical practitioners of all kinds. Elisabeth identified five phases a person goes through when they know they are dying: denial, anger, bargaining, depression, and acceptance. Elisabeth was also instrumental in bringing hospice to the United States from England. This has become a blessing for dying patients and their families.

I was a student nurse before Elisabeth began her work with the dying. A high school student on the ward was dying. He had private nurses, and I asked one of them about him. She told me that he had been an athlete, a swimmer, and that he had gone from weighing 160 pounds to just 75 pounds. He often screamed in pain. I asked the nurse why he wasn't getting his pain medication more often. "I have to follow the doctor's orders," she replied. "We don't want the patient to become addicted." I was horrified at this stupidity. The boy was dying. What difference would it make if he became addicted? If this young boy had hospice care, he would have had relief for his pain, and he would have been able to die at home with his family around him. Hospice is an enormous blessing, especially for people like that boy.

Elisabeth was also vilified for another reason. Some of the dying patients she worked with began appearing to her after they died. They wanted her to understand that death is only a transformation from one way of life to another. They wanted her to tell people that death need not be feared. They taught her that when we die we come into the presence of absolute, unconditional love, and in that presence we review our life—our choices, our decisions, and our actions. Elisabeth had not only insulted medicine by interviewing dying patients, she had also insulted and offended the organized religions that control their members by promising them the salvation and protection that we already have.

The media made fun of her and called her crazy. Elisabeth ignored them and began interviewing people who had near-death experiences. She discovered that people with near-death experiences had similar stories to those patients who had appeared to her after their death.

This is what she learned. When we die, we come into the presence of absolute, unconditional love, and in that presence, we do a life review. God makes each of us unique and incomplete. Life is a school where we learn to grow into who we have been made to be, who we truly are. Learning takes place through the choices we make and the things that we do. All that we learn and every single thing we do is encoded into our being. When we die, we return to God, and in that loving presence we remember what we have learned and what we have done.

When we are born into this life, we experience ourselves as isolated individuals. However, the truth of existence is that we are not separate from the rest of Creation, and when we are in the absolute truth of God's presence, we perceive through God's eyes and experience the wholeness of absolute, unconditional love and that we are a tiny piece of that wholeness. Opposites and opposition no longer exist. We experience the whole of our life, our thoughts and our actions, from the point of view of everyone and everything our life and our choices have touched. Elisabeth told me that as a child she had a difficult time with the idea of a hell where people suffer forever. What she learned from her unearthly visitors is that hell is a reality built from our choices and our actions and exists within us. God is not vengeful. God is unconditional love that entails both mercy and justice.

Imagine Adolf Hitler coming into the presence of total, unconditional love reviewing his life, his actions, and his choices. He would experience the death, the torture, and the suffering of the millions who were impacted by his decisions, a hell of his own making. When he emerged from that hell, he would be an wild old man who was shaped by the suffering of the millions of people his decisions touched. Nothing God has made is wasted or lost. None of us are lost either. All of us are loved, and each of us is accountable for our actions and our choices. When we do our life review, we experience the pain and suffering our actions have caused others, and we suffer as they did. When we become aware of how we have loved and nourished Creation, we learn and rejoice, and Creation rejoices with us. When we have completed our life review, we are shown the infinite possibilities that are there for us to keep learning, and with God's help, we choose another lifetime in order to begin that process again.

When we are born again, we do not remember where we were or why we have come. We are free to choose our destiny, and once again we are shaped and reshaped by our experiences and our actions, growing closer to God and to who we truly are. Even though we experience ourselves as isolated individuals in this life, we are not alone, and the people and the events of the world around us shape our lives. The way we react to this shaping can build us up or tear us down.

Elisabeth told me this story about a family that lived near her. It is great example of the chaotic and transformative effects linked with death and dying. One of the children, a little girl, was dying from leukemia. Her two older brothers became a discipline problem at school and were flunking everything. Their little girl was in a great deal of pain. The parents asked Elisabeth to visit the family and help them deal with their problems.

Elisabeth spoke with the boys individually and learned they were angry because all the attention was focused on their sister. They told Elisabeth that their parents didn't care what happened to them, so they stopped caring about anything too. Elisabeth asked the parents to have a family meeting and taught the family how to bring problems out into the open and then discuss how to solve them. This worked for the family, and things became better.

A month later the mother called Elisabeth and asked her to visit them again and speak with their daughter. The little girl had become terrified of everything, and her parents did not know how to help her. The child was afraid to sleep and afraid to ask for anything for her pain. Elisabeth sat down with the little girl and asked her to draw a picture. Most of her picture was dark black lines over a yellow sun and a blue sky, an image of profound depression.

As the child told Elisabeth about her picture, she remembered a visit from one of the nuns who taught at her school. The little girl told Elisabeth that the sister told her she had to love Jesus more than anything else, so she could get into heaven. The child sobbed and told Elisabeth that she loved her mommy and daddy much more than she loved Jesus, so she would never go to heaven when she died. Elisabeth could not argue with what the nun had told the child, and yet she had to find a way to give the little girl the truth. Elisabeth knew the daughter was an excellent student and that she loved school. Missing school was one of the hardest parts of being home and being sick. Elisabeth thought for a minute and then asked the little girl if her life was a school, and God was her teacher, what kind of things was she learning? The little girl looked down at her skinny body and her swollen belly. "I must be a very bright student because I have been given a really hard lesson," she said. Once the little girl could move through the chaos and terror of what she had been told into an understanding of the truth, she was able to let go of life, and she died two days later.

The slang phrase "go with the flow" captures this cycle of life, death, and transformation. We human beings have a body, a mind, emotions, and sexuality, and we can take action. To be in balance, our minds must be open and receptive, our emotions must give us energy, our bodies must hold our energy, and our ability to act increases or decreases our spiritual development. When our minds are closed, when our emotions are held, and when our sexuality is not linked with our minds and our emotions, we are out of balance. When our behavior is not linked with our emotions, our minds, our bodies, and our sexuality, we are out of balance. When we are out of balance and our life energy is blocked, we produce repetitive life dramas that lower our life energy and lower and block the life energy of others. We can become depressed and create depression in others. The robber, the rapist, the predator, the abuser, the liar, the cheater, the misunderstood one, and the victim are the dramatic roles that are acted out in any drama. Where there is drama, there is depression. The cycles of nature are halted. There is no death and no transformation.

Once I worked with a woman who was very angry with her mother. Her mother shamed her and beat her when she was little. Because her mother was dead, the woman could not tell her how angry she was with her. She decided to write her mother a letter listing all the things that her mother had done to hurt her. It was a long letter.

She read it to me, and I asked her if she had placed all of her pain in the letter, so she could truly let it go. She thought for a while and was sure she had placed all of her pain in the letter and that the best way to let it all go was to burn the letter in my fireplace, so she did. I asked her what she was going to do with the ashes. She said she would leave them in my fireplace. I was not willing to keep her toxic waste in my fireplace. Her pain did not belong to me. She thought about it and then decided to put the ashes in the garbage. I asked her if she thought it was right to give her pain to the garbage men. She thought about it and finally took the ashes and buried them. She planted a small tree on that piece of soil and believed that the tree would grow tall, fertilized by the ashes.

Most of us don't think of our pain as toxic waste, and yet it is. Most nasty and abusive behavior comes from that hurt place within us where someone has been nasty or abusive to us. When we do not face our pain and take responsibility for it, we pass it on. We want to think that life is fair. It is not. How many times have we said or heard someone say, "It's not fair," wanting someone to side with them and blame the perpetrator? Blaming does nothing for us except depress the movement of the cycles of nature and growth in our lives.

CHAPTER TWELVE

Human Attachment

Another way to think of the old Indian man, the old monk and Woman Who Walks in Balance is to look at their relationships. Each of them changed the way they related to the people around them as they began the journey from death into life. There are four ways to have a relationship: secure, avoidant, ambivalent, or chaotic. We use each of these styles in relationship, and most of the time we use them without awareness.

Suffering is manufactured in a relationship when people switch from secure to avoidant or to ambivalent or chaotic ways of relating. The words speak for themselves. Ask yourself questions like,

- When do I avoid telling the truth?

- When do I feel secure telling the truth?

- When do I lie to avoid conflict?

- When do I create chaos and drama to avoid a true connection?

When we have difficulty in a relationship, one of the parties is using one style, usually secure, and then switching the style to create or avoid conflict. Lying creates conflict. Refusing to take responsibility is a form of avoidance. Substance abuse, physical abuse, witnessing abuse, and gambling create chaotic relationships, and when the primary mode of communication is denial, the abuser's family members' ability to think is compromised. That is because family members are blamed for the abuse: "You made me do it, and I have to punish you for it." "You have done this and this and this wrong; therefore, you must be punished." "You know you should stay out of my way when I'm drinking and doping, so I'd better beat that out of your system." Children brought up in this kind of a system develop one of the three human responses to trauma: fight, flight, or freeze. They carry these responses into every relationship.

When we are in a place of death, our emotions, our bodies, our minds, our behavior, and/or our sexuality are held hostage or thwarted in some way. The journey from death into life is to set ourselves free from those things. What does life look like? What does it feel like?

CHAPTER THIRTEEN

Depression, Relationships, and Drama

One of the most difficult courses in our school of life is being in relationship. We are fathers and mothers, sisters and brothers, husbands and wives. We belong to a group, a profession, a color, a culture, a school, a city, a state, and a nation. We love, we hate, we get angry, ashamed, and afraid, and sometimes all at once. Most of what we do is in relationship with someone or something. Most of the time it is not hard to be in relationship with something because the something doesn't talk back or give us a hard time. Being in relationship with someone runs the gamut from super hard to fairly easy depending upon how close we are. The dramatic leveler in any relationship is the emotional intensity involved.

The old Indian man and the old monk were out of sync with themselves and with the Spirit. Woman Who Walks in Balance was pushed from being in sync into being totally cut off from anything but hate and rage. She had to choose to earn and learn to be back in sync. Most of us are a mixture with parts of us in sync and parts of us far from balanced. All of us will get hurt in one or more relationships. All of us will have to work hard to maintain a relationship. The word "love" has many meanings, from what is in our own heart to what the expectations are in our culture. Love is a school where we learn to give, to receive, to communicate, and to listen. We are shaped to be in relationship in our first few years of life in the way we attach to other human beings. This shaping is dependent upon our own unique bio—chemistry, the kind of parenting we receive, and the level of nastiness in the people around us. The results are that we feel secure or ambivalent, avoidant or chaotic in relationship. How does that look?

We come into relationship with an attachment style. In order to stay in relationship, we must learn to change our attachment style. to

How do we become awake and aware? By turning inward and reflecting upon our experience. Keeping a journal is one way to begin this process. A journal is like a diary. In the journal, we record the events of our daily lives, including our dreams, our successes, and our mistakes. When we turn inward and reflect upon what we have experienced, we begin a process that activates deeper levels of our being that carry the potential for awareness. Turning inward and developing a relationship with ourselves is just as important as developing relationships with other people.

A four-year-old boy comes into a health clinic because he screams and bangs his head against the wall in pre-school. He is physically fine, well-nourished, and doing the things normal four-year-olds do. As part of his evaluation, he is sent to an art therapist who asks him to draw a picture. His picture is full of black and red colors with jagged teeth. The art therapist goes to her supervisor and says she believes the child is in trouble at home. The nurse at the clinic does a home visit and discovers that the boy was scalped by his mother's boyfriend when he was two years of age. He was taken away from his mother and given to his grandmother.

They discovered his grandmother was an alcoholic who would tie him to a chair when she went out drinking. She was very careful about not staying out too long or going too far from home, but the child had no sense of time and struggled to escape his bonds until he finally fell asleep. The child was taken away from the grandmother and placed in a foster home. He was never seen again at that clinic.

Human beings are resilient. That little boy may have grown up with his soul looking something like his picture; however, he did not have to become that way. His attachment style was probably as chaotic as his surroundings, but perhaps not. When he becomes mature, he can learn to change if he can become aware of it. It reminds me of a Buddhist sutra, a wise saying: "The deeper the mud, the more beautiful the bloom on the lotus."

CHAPTER FOURTEEN

The Tools for Leaving the Drama

Breath

The first thing we do when we are born into this life is take a breath. The last thing we do before we die is take a final breath. Breath is linked with spirit and vitality. In the days when midwives were the primary people delivering babies, the breath of life was sacred and considered to be part of the breath of God. The midwife would breathe into the baby's mouth to honor God for the gift of life. At the end of life, the midwife cared for the dying person and took in their last breath to give the person back to God.

Breath underwrites our drama because it is a constant. Each of us must learn how our breath supports our negative drama.

Developing an Awareness of Breath

Our breath is a visible extension of our vitality, our spirit. When we are caught in a negative drama, our breath is held captive and is no longer vital. Babies breathe perfectly, and we can learn from them. If you watch a baby breathe, you will notice that the baby's belly extends out on the inhale and drops back down to a neutral position on the exhale. Learning to become aware of our breath is essential to letting go of drama. There are many ways we can become aware of our breath.

Breath is one of the everyday ways we move from the death of being caught in a drama into a life that is rich in energy and full of possibilities. If we were aware of being caught, we would no longer be caught. When we finally throw up our hands and surrender to the truth of what we are doing, we must die to the sweet lies we have told ourselves to shift the blame for our painful circumstances away from us. Breath is the key that opens us up to what is closed and hidden from us. Our breath is the key that opens the door to awareness.

To use your breath, we must face the fact that we are the one directing our drama, and we are the only one who has the power to change it. It is breath that connects us to our bodies. Our bodies do not lie, and it is breath that connects us with our body.

Breathing Like a Baby

Lie down on your back, and extend your belly outward as you inhale. This extension drops the diaphragm, so your lungs can take in more air. Allow your belly to go back to neutral as you exhale. Once you feel comfortable breathing this way, begin practicing upright while walking. The center of the body is about one to two finger widths below the belly button. Begin breathing into that center as you walk. Let the breath pull you along while you exhale. It is fun to walk this way and a wonderful way to learn about breath.

Breath can become prayer. Inhale the light and exhale the dark. This is another way to meditate. Breath and meditation go hand in hand when we become aware of how to breathe.

Embryonic Breathing

Begin the next kind of breathing lying down. Imagine a pole is standing on the horizon. Imagine another pole standing up straight from the place that is one to two finger widths below your belly button. Inhale and then imagine a golden cord of light coming up from within you and climbing the pole. Exhale and imagine the cord of light moving out toward the pole on the horizon. Stop breathing and imagine the golden cord circling the far pole. Inhale and imagine the golden cord of light coming back to the pole coming from your low belly. Stop breathing while you imagine the golden cord circling the pole and then exhale, sending the golden cord back to the far pole. Still not breathing, imagine the golden cord circling the far pole. Inhale and imagine the golden cord returning to the pole extending from your lower belly. Pause and do not breathe. Imagine the golden cord going around the pole connected to your lower belly. Exhale and imagine the golden cord returning to the pole on the horizon. Stop breathing and imagine the golden cord going around the pole on the horizon. Inhale and imagine the golden cord returning to the pole at your low belly. Do not breathe as you imagine the golden cord going around the pole at your low belly. Exhale and imagine the golden cord returning to the pole standing on the horizon. When you feel you have successfully completed nine rotations, imagine the golden cord returning its place inside your low belly.

Meditation

Meditation is the practice of focusing the mind on something for a specific amount of time. It is a practice rooted in ancient times, and there are hundreds of ways to do it. Embryonic breathing is one example of meditation. Linked with meditation is "mindfulness." When we practice mindfulness, we attempt to do everything to the best of our ability with a sense of peace and relaxation. When we are not focused on what we do, we make mistakes. Our mistakes can be our greatest teachers if we are willing to learn from them as well as from the mistakes of others—including our teachers.

Rotate Chi

This is a timed meditation. Start meditating for five minutes, and gradually increase the meditation time to twenty minutes. Sit straight up using no support for your back unless absolutely necessary. Place your tongue behind your teeth at the roof of your mouth. Place your hands palm down in your lap. Smile to help your body relax.

This form of meditation focuses on five places: on the center of the top of the head, just above the center of the eyebrows, on the tip of the nose, on the chin, and on the large bone at the back of the neck.

Begin by focusing on the center of your head. Move your attention down to the center just above your eyebrows. Now move your attention down to the tip of your nose. Move your attention down to your chin. Finally, move your attention to the bone at the back of your neck.

When I started this practice, I pressed each area with a fingernail, so I could truly feel the places. If I had trouble focusing, I counted to twenty to keep my focus. Gradually, I was able to stop the counting and the pressing.

When you are finished, move your arms up in front of you as if you were hugging someone. Separate your arms as if you were pulling them apart from a hug. Drop your elbows, and place your hands up with your palms at ear level facing forward, and push your hands out slowly, making a hissing sound. Keep your hands in the same position. Pull your hands back, and extend your palms quickly, as if you were pushing someone in the chest. Imagine energy coming from your low belly and expelling it as you extend your hands quickly and with a low voice say, "HA." Keep pulling your hands back, pushing forward, and saying "HA" until you feel all the energy is released.

Understanding Your Breath in Drama and Depression

Place yourself in a quiet, comfortable space. Practice embryonic breathing until you feel comfortably relaxed. Review the "Getting to Know Yourself" assessment. Read through your response, and if you begin to feel uncomfortable, take note of your breathing and your posture. Change your breathing back to the pattern of breathing like a baby. Pay attention to how long it takes you to relax. Do this exercise until you are thoroughly familiar with how your breathing changes between relaxation and drama. The goal of this exercise is to learn to interrupt the breathing pattern of the drama and change it using your breath, so you finally have a choice to move out of the drama at will.

Intent

Leaving a drama requires preparation. How you are leaving, when you are leaving, what you are changing, and where you are going are important factors in exiting a drama.

Intent is directly linked with the mind, and it is that part of us that supports change. To develop your intent, pick something that you wish to change. Start with something small. To create change, you must let go of something and decide what you want to hang on to. As you work with intent, increase the level of difficulty after each success.

For example, if you decide to meditate, start slowly, and meditate for five minutes. To begin, relax and sink your attention down to that place in your body just below the navel. This is the physical location for intent. Invisible fibers come out from that center and connect us with the past, the present, the future, the world around us, and the Creator. Then do the meditation itself.

Yielding

Another way to make changes is by yielding what you wish to change to the Creator. One of the great places to begin using yielding is when you are standing in line and feeling in a hurry. Feel the impatience, then make an image of the physical sensation and give it to God. "Dear God, I give this impatience to you. I ask you to lift it from me and then fill the empty places within me with your presence, your wisdom, your strength, and your love."

Chanting

There is a beautiful Buddhist chant called "Nam Miyōhō Renge Kyō." It comes from the Lotus Sutra, the last of the Buddha's teachings. Chanting was developed to ease human suffering and help people rise above suffering by making them wiser. The core message of the chant means the one chanting can attain enlightenment without restrictions in this lifetime.

To begin chanting, sit facing a blank wall, and make yourself comfortable. Put your hands together in a prayer position over your heart. Keep your eyes open. Chant on one note and then concentrate on the sounds, "Nam Miyōhō Renge Kyō." Chant for as long as you feel comfortable, and chant whenever you wish for as long as you wish.

Prayer

Young Navajo girls spoke the following prayer after their moon courses began and they were initiated into the community of women:

> Oh Great Spirit whose voice I hear in the wind
> let me stand before you naked and unashamed
> with my shadow at my feet.
> Teach me to walk in beauty: with beauty before me
> and beauty behind me, with beauty to the right of me
> and beauty to the left of me, with beauty above me
> and beauty below me.
> Teach me to walk in beauty, so I perceive
> your presence and your ways and embody your
> wisdom.

These women birthed the children, cared for the young, made the clothes, butchered the meat, grew the crops, gathered the harvest, and cooked and preserved the food. They were the glue that held the community together. Can you imagine doing all of these things and being mindful enough to do them beautifully? If these young women were faithful to their prayer, their mindset would foster secure attachments.

In the Navajo prayer, the young woman asks to "stand naked and unashamed" before the Great Spirit and then ask that her shadow lie at her feet. "Shadow" is a powerful word. The image of shadow comes from standing in the light and noticing that we cast a shadow. In psychological terms, our shadow is what we do not wish to be aware of, our greedy, lustful, lying, raging, fearful, self-important, self-pitying parts. We can also have a light shadow that holds gifts and talents we are not aware of. When we are not aware, we act from these places, hurting ourselves and hurting others, just like the old monk at the gate to the monastery that I told you about earlier.

Bloom Where You Are Planted, Eileen

Eileen was one of the most beautiful people I have ever met. She was one of the last living people to get Bulbar polio. She was fifteen at that time. Her greatest physical accomplishment was learning to breathe outside an iron lung. She was paralyzed from the neck down.

In her early twenties, she had a spiritual experience that changed her. She told me that until that time she was a "shut in." After her experience she was changed into a woman who could listen to others and help them.

Her family broke due to guilt when she became paralyzed. She lived with her father, but her mom and her siblings moved away. As an adult, she had to rely on social security disability payments. I know this because she would get a letter from the state every so often suggesting she belonged in a nursing home rather than getting care at home.

Eileen hired teenagers to care for her and trained them. The young people she hired were on the brink of delinquency, and caring for her brought them back to solid ground. She had to be fed. She had to have an enema three times a week. She had a catheter. She had a special telephone with a microphone that she could turn on by tapping her head against it. The young people who cared for her saw hardship that they had never dreamed of and a bravery they wanted to copy. If she had been forced into a nursing home, I think she would have died. The great good she did for the young people who cared for her cannot be measured.

Word got out about her, and several years before she died, a group of young (sixteen- and seventeen-year-olds) "born again Christians" visited her. They asked if they could pray over her for healing. At that time Eileen had been paralyzed for over twenty-two years. Her bones were brittle from lack of weight-bearing exercise, and she probably weighed about eighty pounds. The young people prayed over her and then grabbed her and sat her up to "claim the healing." They let go of her, and she dropped back into bed, wrenching her back and joints.

They glared at her and told her that she was not healed because she had a demon and that she had a demon because she had no faith. Then they left. Eileen called me to tell me what had happened and asked me to come over and help her. She was in pain, and she was also upset. The very foundation of her belief and trust in God had been shaken. It took her quite awhile to settle back into trusting in God and God's purpose for her.

Those teenagers were the first "levitated" people I ever met. They read the Bible instead of doing drugs and were very proud of that. They believed the words they read, taking them literally, and believed they had been given the gift of healing. Then they hustled over to Eileen to claim the truth of the words they had read. There was just one problem. They had no understanding of healing. They certainly did not stop to question Eileen about what she thought about their methods, and they were too ignorant to understand the true healing that took place through a wounded woman whose life's work was to "bloom where she was planted." Eileen recovered spiritually from the experience, but she lived in great pain until she died.

Several years later, Eileen was hospitalized with congestive heart failure. She knew she was dying, so she asked one of the caregivers she had brought with her to the hospital to call all her friends and ask them to come to the hospital to say goodbye.

When I arrived, about twenty people were in the waiting room. I went in to see Eileen. She asked me to hold her, so I climbed into bed with her and held her. She told me that she wasn't scared to die anymore. She had one tether left holding her to life, and that was saying goodbye to her friends. "If I don't die today, I'm going to feel like a real asshole for asking all these people to come to say goodbye," she said. We laughed. She died ten hours later.

Letting Go of Ego, Self-Importance, and Self-Pity

The ego is not the center of our consciousness. Think about that for a minute. We know we store most of our experience somewhere in our mind. We know we don't remember most of it unless we need to. Where does it go? Where does the sense that we are an ongoing being come from?

Carl Jung, along with Sigmund Freud and Alfred Adler, was one of the first people to think about human beings as psychological in nature. All three of these men were troubled by how little we know about ourselves. They are the fathers of modern psychology. Psychology is an infant science compared to the science of mathematics, and even today, we humans are a mystery to ourselves. Jung observed the ways in which people reacted to stress and pain and developed ways to identify what he called complexes. I have used the word "drama" to describe them. Complexes are repetitive dramas that have a physical, emotional, and mental cohesiveness. A complex can override consciousness and behave independently. It is not a part of the ego.

Jung wondered where complexes came from. He also studied hundreds of dreams, and he found that dreams also did not come from the ego. He believed a "dream maker" lives within us and orders our dreaming and waking experiences. However, if the ego does not order dreaming or create complexes, what does? Jung struggled with this question.

At that time he had a friend in China who was being initiated as a Taoist monk. As they shared ideas, his friend gave him a different perspective on human psychology. The Taoist classic *Tao Te Ching* was written around 650 bc by Lao Tzu. "Tao" means God, "Te" is the little part of God within us, and "Ching" is the story of the relationship between Tao and Te. Jung realized that the Te lives within us and is the author of dreams and complexes. He called this author the "self." The self is a little piece of God within a human being, the part of us that travels from lifetime to lifetime, gathering experience and learning. It is the part of us that connects us to God.

We are born with an ego, an "I am." It is the part of us that learns and grows, the part of us that does the grocery shopping and pays the bills. The ego of a child is selfish and self-absorbed, needy and dependent, filled with expectations, very demanding, and often manipulative to get what it wants.

In children the ego is enormous, which is normal and correct. As a child matures the ego becomes relativized to the point that what is not ego—what is other, not oneself—can be received, respected, and empathized with. Can you imagine a two-year-old with empathy?

The ego is the part of us that manages your checkbook, drives your car, and does the grocery shopping and the work of journaling. When the ego is inflated or filled with self-pity, we regress to childlike immaturity and are filled with self-importance, competitiveness, expectations, attachments, greed, fear, rage, and self-pity. We lack empathy and respect. This is the shadow spoken of in the Navajo prayer. Letting go of our immaturity and becoming aware of our tendency toward nastiness is the true journey from death into life.

Our consciousness is layered into two levels: conscious and unconscious. One level of the unconscious contains all the things we have lived and forgotten. It is called the "personal unconscious." The second layer is called the "collective unconscious." This level contains the experiences of our ancestors back to the beginning of human awareness. These two levels are intertwined. When we take time to reflect upon our experience and journal about it, our beauty, our faults, and our sins enter our conscious awareness. When we turn inward and face our sin, we can focus on what is positive and possible for us to take in. God can nourish us, and when we are truly nourished, our faults are squeezed out; we simply have no room for them. This is true not only for us; it must also be truth for our partner. Each of us must "walk our talk" whether we are in relationship or not.

When we feel empowered in a relationship, when we are free to learn and develop, and when we feel respected, the relationship is healthy. If the partners are not working together, the relationship will fail. In our country one in seven men and one in four women experience some form of domestic violence each year. The divorce rate is about 38 percent for first-time marriages. What kind of dedication does it take to remain faithful and loving when it is almost impossible to do so?

CHAPTER FIFTEEN

The Gentle Art of Self-Defense

When we know ourselves and how to defend ourselves, we no longer fear or are victimized by the tyrants around us.

When I was forty-three years old, I had problems with my back. My back would move out of alignment, and when it did, the muscles around the misalignment would go into spasm. It got so bad that sometimes I was in bed for weeks at a time in a back brace and on muscle relaxants. The physician who was treating me suggested a spinal fusion, placing a metal plate in my back to hold the bones together. I researched the complications associated with the surgery and found that over 45 percent of people who had the surgery had chronic pain. I knew that our medical system does not deal well with chronic pain. I thought about it and what made sense to me was to build up the muscles in my back, so my muscles would act like a metal plate.

It was 1983, and I could not find anyone to help me build up those muscles. At that time three of my children were studying martial arts. They said their teacher could help me, and he did. For three years I practiced a series of eighteen movements. I had to start slowly because I had not exercised since high school. I began practicing for twenty minutes a day and gradually increased to ninety minutes a day. It was very painful, but over time my body healed. The practice captivated me and was very difficult. No one coddled me or felt sorry for me. I stood in line behind my children. Some of the students made fun of me and called me an "edi-cated" woman and looked down on me for being so lacking in physical skills. No one could do the work but me, so I made that place and that time sacred and decided that whatever happened to me, good or bad, was a learning experience. I had no idea that this idea is another royal road from death into life. This stance of making the situation we are in the absolute truth is one of the truths of life. The martial arts school had a saying: "You make yourself good. You make yourself bad." Movement combined with meditation was another royal road for the everyday journey from death into life.

As I practiced, I realized that when I practiced, I was in a meditative state. That is because I had to relax, so I did not injure myself. I was taught to relax and sink my attention into the space two inches below the belly button. This space is the center of the body, and all movement comes from there. Remember the breathing exercises? When we move from this space, the movement alters our breathing, and the breath moves our body. Even though I was practicing martial arts, I was learning to relax in a way that felt feminine and yielding rather than harsh and constricted like punching and kicking. Doing movement as a meditation was and is amazing. Over the years I have played with this experience, and I invite you to do the same.

Part of martial arts training is expecting conflict. There are five steps for dealing with conflict: 1) be careful where you go and when you go; 2) run away; 3) protect your body; 4) injure quickly, then move away; 4) maim, and 5) kill. These principles are the rules for the gentle art of self-defense.

The treasure hidden within the tyrant teachings is an acceptance that produces readiness and self-preservation. Our Judeo–Christian heritage teaches us to turn the other cheek and to love our enemies. Reality dic-tates that we remove our cheek and then love from a distance.

CHAPTER SIXTEEN

Becoming Awake and Aware

Life

In graduate school we were required to do a thesis. The Berwyn-Cicero council on aging was close to the hospital where I was teaching. I was very interested in how people over age sixty-five thought about the world and what was important to them. Over one thousand people were seen there every week. It also had a staff of volunteers who worked with the people: feeding, washing, organizing events, and overseeing safety and transportation. I wanted to interview healthy elderly people, so I asked the staff to help me find som. I told them I wanted to ask the group about their opinions regarding death, intimacy, religion, and how the world around them had changed. The people selected would be interviewed, but their names would not ever be made public. They had their basic needs met: physiological (basic survival needs), they were safe, able to socialize, had a sense of self-esteem, and were learning and growing.

The staff found twenty people who were willing to be interviewed. Next, I asked the staff to identify ten of these people who were flexible, free thinking, had integrity, were capable of intimacy, autonomous, and who enjoyed life. They came up with ten volunteers.

Each interview took an hour. I asked the subjects to be as honest as possible with me. The group that was identified as having the most fun gave the best interviews. They were very open and honest. One man told me that he and his wife had purchased their graves at a beautiful cemetery with mature trees and a small lake. Once in a while they picnicked on that site and, after eating, they danced on the graves.

Another woman told me that her husband died of prostate cancer. Several months before he died, he went out and bought a puppy. She told me that he was a real "bastard" because he knew she would want to die and follow him, but she wouldn't be able to because she would have to take care of the puppy.

Everyone in the "happy group" had some sort of spiritual experience, whether they attended church or not. One man told me that he had had visions for years and that, as a result, he believed he was to help anyone who crossed his path. He told me story after story about the people he had helped. Most of those people never knew that it was him who had helped them. None of the people in the happy group were afraid to talk about death, and all of them had wills and funeral arrangements already made.

They taught me that living a full life means embracing our situation and all that is around us. It means letting go of what does not nourish us. It means choosing to be happy and really being happy, smiling rather than frowning, and being grateful for what is here. Most of them told me that happiness is a choice, and the choice brings peace and joy. They also spoke of integrity and how important it is to never to lie to ourselves.

The other ten people in the first group were more traditional and bound by a code of conduct that was centered on what other people thought of them as well as rules and laws that their religion or family taught them and what they thought was normal. Most were resentful, feeling that life had dealt with them harshly and unfairly.

There were two exceptions in this group. One woman divorced her husband, who was an abusive alcoholic, and raised two children by herself. She lost her friends because they all drank and judged her harshly for divorcing her husband. (At that time, divorce was not an option for women.) Her suffering made her self-reliant and very independent. She decided she would never marry again or subject herself to any man. (From the 1930s, to the 1950s, the cultural norm was that women stayed home and took care of children, and the man was the provider and the final authority on everything that went on in the home).

The second exception in this group was a man who had never married. He told me he was never attracted to women, but homosexuality was not an option for him because it was considered a sin in his religion. He had never spoken about this to anyone. He told me that he had learned to be alone and like it.

Closed Off and Boxed In

Many of us are numb, dull, and blind. We work, come home, and watch TV. Things in our daily life are predictable and comfortable, and we like it that way. We are mentally blank and emotionally dull. Real emotions pass quickly, but we carry with us an emotional theme based on fear, anger, or shame. We are depressed.

Periodically, a drama comes into our life, invented or invited, and we either overcome it or endure it. Sometimes we may wonder if that's all there is because we are so closed off and boxed in. We are caught in a "living death," and we will stay in that place unless we decide to leave it. How do we begin to do this?

The desire to become awake and aware is built into us, and becoming aware is the everyday journey from death (ignorance, fear, hate, and greed) into life. Part of that journey is learning to work with ourselves emotionally, physically, mentally, sexually, and spiritually through action and non-action, through opening and then closing. The ways we work with our human aspects are described below.

Behavior

Our behavior makes us grow or stops our growth, and it has everything to do with our everyday journey from death into life.

Emotions

Emotions flow like water and give us energy. They are part and parcel of what it is to be a human being. When we do not express them, we damage our bodies. When we express them as we experience them, we can damage others or ourselves. When we are mature, we neither implode nor explode when we experience a strong emotion. What can we do with our emotions? How can we cooperate with them and learn to flow with them? First we must become aware of them and then accept them. Once we have accepted them, it is important to relax into them.

An emotion does not last long. Attachment to an emotion can become a theme that lasts for the rest of our lives. (A drama is held together by an emotional theme.) Once we are aware and accepting, we can use emotional energy to create, to sing, to move our bodies, and to write music, stories, songs, and poetry. We can paint them and use words to describe them in a journal or share them with others. Sometimes we can pray to be released from them.

Human beings have nine innate motions[4]

Neutrality

Interest----------Excitement

Startle-----------Surprise

Distress---------Anguish

Enjoyment------Joy

---

4   Sylvan Tompkins developed this theory about affect in 1962

Fear------------Terror

Anger-----------Rage

Disgust---------Contempt

Shame----------Humiliation

I remember coming home after a difficult meeting with someone. During the meeting I could not speak, only listen. The woman I was meeting with was very angry with me. I felt as if the whole front of my body had been punctured with darts laced with rage. I arrived home and told my husband what had happened and asked him for help. He told me to go upstairs (where I had a little altar) and pray. As soon as I began praying, I knew I had to forgive the person who hurt me, and as I prayed, I felt a release from the pain.

I practiced as an analyst/therapist for almost forty years. One of my first patients was a woman who was filled with rage and unaware of it. After our first session, I vomited. I knew that if I wanted to continue to practice, I needed supervision with an experienced analyst. I worked with Peter M. throughout my analytic training and continued working with him until I retired. We discussed my physical sensitivity and decided the best way to approach it was to tape two patient sessions and go over the tapes while under supervision and address my sensations during sessions. I asked the patients I was going to tape for permission and told them why I wanted to record them. I promised their names and history would never be disclosed. This was about me, not them. They graciously agreed to help me.

My closest friend, Mary Loomis, died from breast cancer. After Mary died, I called a colleague, Lucy K., who had survived breast cancer. She told me that Mary called her and asked Lucy how she survived. Lucy told Mary that she stopped seeing patients. "I could never do that," Marry told her. "Where would the love come from?" I understood then that

Mary nurtured her patients, and they nurtured her in return. The negative affect present in the relational field had never been dealt with.

An invisible relational field exists in human relationships. Emotions are present and can be stored in this field. When we become aware of our emotions, it is easier to understand what kind of field we are in at any given moment. When the field depletes our energy, it is time to make changes in the relationship or let the relationship go.

Memory is linked to emotion. We do not remember what is not linked with emotion. Math has no emotion; however, a person who loves math can remember the longest equations, and someone who does not love math will remember very little.

Body

Our body is the earth of our being, and like the earth, our body holds energy. If you have ever held a stone in your hand shortly after sundown, you will feel the warmth of the sun in the stone. Our bodies also hold emotional energy.

Physical exercise is very important to keep the body healthy. My experience has been that, after age fifty, pounding the joints by jogging and running or locking the joints with heavy weightlifting damages the body. It is important to do some kind of aerobic exercise, lift light weights with high repetitions, and do yoga to maintain strength and flexibility. It is also important to move our internal energy or chi.

Chinese monks observed the world around them and realized that the body holds energy, just like earth holds the sun's heat. Chi circulates throughout the body following the blood. The Chinese have mapped out channels and meridians for centuries. When the normal circulation of chi is blocked, the result is disease. Acupuncture can be used to treat the blockages. However, these disciplines work with the body internally to develop chi and promote the flow of chi: Tai chi, Bagua, and Xing Yi and some forms of meditation also build up this internal energy. Embryonic breathing is one of those exercises. Another is the rotate chi described in a previous chapter.

When the chi is finally purified, the person turns into light, a sign that they are enlightened. Building internal energy requires being truthful and practicing virtue. Pride, greed, lust, anger, gluttony, envy, and laziness deplete our energy.

Taoism and the requirements for tai chi practice went in and out of favor in China, depending on the ever-changing political climate. To protect their teachings, the monks placed their knowledge of how to build chi into the martial arts. In India the practice of yoga was used to strengthen and build life energy.

In our culture, we are familiar with how to strengthen our bodies with exercise, but few of us have learned how to strengthen ourselves internally, and that ignorance allows us to be taken advantage of by western medicine, pharmaceutical companies, and fad exercises or physical training that injures rather than helps.

You can study yoga and Tai chi by buying DVDs. What is important to know about these practices is the breathing you do while practicing. Tai chi should be practiced very slowly. You can increase your focus by using your imagination to picture the Tai chi ball as light coming out of your midsection (that place below your navel where your "intent" resides, the dan tien) onto your palms and sticking to your palms as you move. When you separate your hands, imagine a large ball of light between them and as you move through the postures. When your hands separate, imagine the large ball splitting into two smaller balls, one on each palm and then coalescing into a large ball when you bring your palms together and when you move your palms to your low dan tien to put the Play with your Tai chi while you imagine your energy. The Chinese speak of 'playing Tai Chi' because during the practice the body must be as relaxed as a newborn child. When you feel comfortable practicing this way, you can add embryonic breathing to your practice as you inhale and exhale. Your focus and your practice will improve. You do not need to perform many postures. Narrow your focus down to twelve postures, and concentrate on those. This probably sounds overwhelming, but if you break everything down into parts and start small, your concentration will improve, and so will your practice. It is also important to smile during your practice. Smiling helps the body relax.

Mind

The mind is that part of us that is like the wind. The mind receives energy. We can be open minded and receptive or closed minded and blocked, and we can manipulate and be manipulated mentally.

When your mind is blocked, you are opinionated and locked into only one frame of reference, and anything outside of that is considered wrong, bad, or even evil. Moral and ethical judgments as well as prejudice abound, and compassion is lacking. The person with a closed mind is dogmatic and holds inflexibly to tradition. This person is also easily manipulated.

This is a simple example of a closed rule-bound mind. A daughter was placing a sirloin roast in a pan, but before she placed it in the pan, she cut off both ends. Her mother asked why she did that, and the daughter said that was the way she saw her mother do it. The mother laughed and said the reason she cut off both ends of the big roasts was because her roasting pan was too small.

When your mind is open, you can view the world from multiple viewpoints. You can develop intent to the point that you can follow through with what you do. You can "walk your talk" and not say one thing and do another. You can call upon multiple resources when needed, and your worldview will be more comprehensive. With an open mind, you are able to "count coup."

How do we develop our minds? We must hold our tongues and learn to listen, observe, and ask questions. When we are speaking, we are communicating our point of view about something. We blather along but learn nothing. Using our tongues can also tear us down when we tear others down by lying, gossiping, or slandering. Questions are better than answers.

Mindfulness

The practice of meditation can be carried into daily to life with mindfulness and is not only required but also simple to do. To be mindful means to put your full attention into what you are doing and to do it as perfectly as possible. When you are mindful, you are at peace, and your mind is not scattered. You are simply doing what you are doing with your full attention. When your attention wanders, pull it back and pay attention to what you are doing.

Sexuality

This is a very sensitive subject in our culture because it is attached to strong emotions linked with archaic rules and laws. Our nation has the highest rate of teenage pregnancies in the world. Statistically, one woman is raped every two minutes in this county, and one out of every ten rape victims is male. Sexually transmitted diseases are epidemic.

I worked with individuals and couples in my therapeutic/analytic practice, but I felt too ignorant to teach couples how to improve their sex lives. The only resource I could find regarding solid sexual information was Harley Swiftdeer Reagan, a half-Native American man who was a gifted teacher. When he talked about his early beginnings, he described being hated by the native Americans because he was white and being hated by the whites because he was native American.

I met him in 1987 when he came to Michigan to do a workshop. Mary Loomis had attended a previous workshop with him and invited me to come to Michigan to attend this workshop with her. "Swift" taught almost non-stop from 11:00 a.m. to 2 a.m. We had a few breaks. He smoked Jakarta cigarettes endlessly and drank Dr. Pepper.

He was a veteran of Vietnam, a sergeant who did night "recon." He was injured several times and came home with a steel plate in his head and severe pain. He knew he needed help and sought it from the head of the Navajo Nation, Tom "Two Bears" Wilson, and then later from Chuck Storm, an author who was also half-Native American. Part of the teachings dealt with sexuality. What was important to me was that these teachings came from a matriarchal lineage not contaminated by western prudery.

Before I discuss the teachings, I want to say to those who call Swift a "pretender" or say he never met Tom "Two Bears" Wilson, my experience was that I spent five days on the reservation with Swift. A Hogan there was reserved for Swift and his students. We brought the people blankets and gifts as a thank-you for sharing their land with us. They were gracious. I felt very welcome. Two Bears was dead by that point, so I did not meet him. However, it was clear to me that a longstanding relationship existed between the Navajo people on that reservation and Swift. He taught me about matriarchal societies.

The biggest difference I found between a matriarchy and a patriarchy is that of hierarchy. Patriarchy is dependent on a hierarchical order. The higher a person's level, the more important he or she is. A matriarchy is based on mutual cooperation. The hierarchy shifts according to who is more qualified to make decisions that affect the tribe. The people know and honor the Creator and do not need a law to remind them of that. There are sacred laws, the first of which is "Honor the woman, for all things are born from the feminine seeded by the masculine." The second sacred law is "Do nothing to harm the children." These two laws make absolute sense. For example, how is a woman who has been genitally mutilated going to nurture her children? How can a powerful patriarchal church teach that a person can only have intercourse with the intention of having a child? These patriarchal laws are based upon power and control rather than respect and common sense.

The sexual teachings that Swift brought to the world begin with the word RESPECT. I used capital letters for because that is how important respect is in any relationship, but especially in a sexual relationship.

My husband and I attended two Quodoushka workshops given by Swift in Michigan. There were rules. In the first workshop, no sexual activity was permitted. The second workshop permitted private sexual activity with only the partner we brought. I will share part of the teachings with you, as I did with the couples I worked with.

First, sexual behavior is sacred, the most powerful energy we possess. It moves our emotions, our mind, our body, and our spirit and can increase the level of energy in these four aspects of being human. When a child in a tribe with this tradition comes into puberty, that child (with his or her consent) is initiated sexually by a teacher of the opposite gender. In the past, before the white Christians took children off the reservation to be educated in white schools, women knew the herbs that prevented conception. That knowledge was lost.

It is important to know and understand how our bodies work. Women have two places to achieve orgasm, the clitoris and the G spot. The G spot is in the vagina about a quarter to a third of the way in on one side. It feels like a round, warty spot. The farther the clitoris is from the vaginal opening, the longer it takes for a woman to have an orgasm. What works sometimes for that is the use of a vibrator along with intercourse.

Men have differing lengths and thicknesses of the penis, which makes things even more complicated. Look at your genitals, and then look at your partner's genitals to see how well they match up.

If you want to be an athlete, you must train. If you want to be good at something, you must practice. Yet we assume that our sexual encounters should be satisfying without knowledge or practice. This is simply not so. The women I worked with in couples therapy often complained about the man being unwilling to take his time. When he learned to slow down, sexual relations improved. The women were expecting their husbands to read their minds and simply know what would satisfy them. Talking together and practicing together will greatly improve your sexual encounters.

Here is an example of an insensitive man. His wife has worked for hours taking care of three toddlers. Meanwhile, he has spent the day fantasizing about their sexual encounter. He comes home from work feeling amorous and finds his wife is exhausted. He presses her to be sexual with him, but she says she is too tired. He continues to press, and they end up having sex. He has his orgasm but does not take her needs into consideration. She is filled with resentment. All she wants is a glass of wine and sleep.

It is helpful to talk about these things and figure out how each partner can get his or her needs met. Practice and play rather than use "quickies" as sexual encounters. It is okay to take your time. It is okay to practice, to explore, and to learn.

Men have their hands on their genitals as soon as they are born. Women do not. A great way for a woman to become more aware of her body is to use a vibrator alone and then graduate to using it when her mate is present.

After intercourse the man leaves energetic particles in the vagina. These particles create an attachment to the male that reduces the female's autonomy. It is important for women to remove these particles from their bodies to protect her independence. Sometime after the sexual encounter, the woman must "sweep" these particles away. Here is an exercise to do that.

Replay the sexual encounter in your mind. Get comfortable with the images from the encounter. Place the images on your right side, and breathe them in. Turn your head to the left, and exhale the images. Repeat this exercise until the images are gone.

Close the exercise facing forward and exhaling with a "Ha!"

Ignorance and lack of communication about sex is one of the roots of divorce. Many women have told me that their husbands are so insensitive during sex that the women write grocery lists or think of people's telephone numbers because the sexual encounter is so one-sided. This can lead to depression. What I am describing is not at all respectful, but it is quite common.

I have had women in my practice who will not take any action to change sexual encounters that they loathe. That is because they believe sex is dirty, and they want no part of it. What is hard about this is that such women make it perfectly clear to their husbands that he can't get it right, or they fake an orgasm to get the encounter over with. Such women have changed their relationships into a parent-child dynamic and are unhappy and unsettled in a position where they have made themselves powerless victims in a drama that can lead to depression. If you want your sexual relationship to be successful, practice, communicate, and be respectful.

There are four levels of orgasm. A man starts at level one, which is physical release. A woman starts at level two because she has two places for orgasm. She needs physical, non-sexual closeness and sharing feelings before and after sex. I have heard many men say they are not interested in "bullshit" feelings; they just want to "come." These men are missing out on higher levels of orgasm.

The third level of orgasm is when couples dream together and develop higher levels of energy. Think about the fact that there are unlimited possibilities in life for exploration, growth, creativity, and learning. When you are depressed, you lack energy for any of these things.

The fourth level of orgasm is merger. The couple merges physically, mentally, and spiritually. They are entwined in God, perceiving the evolution of Creation.

Sexual intercourse or even sexual activity energizes our minds, our emotions, and our bodies. Women entering menopause need an orgasm at least once a week. Not only is it pleasurable, it maintains emotional balance, bone density, flexibility, and mental and spiritual health.

CHAPTER SEVENTEEN

A Ceremony for Forgiveness

In this context, a ceremony is a rite that is performed in a particular way to unite the practitioner or the person attending the ceremony with the spiritual dimension. It increases our energy and helps us unite with sacred mystery.

Weddings, funerals, baptisms, confirmations, bar and bat mitzvahs (moving from childhood into adulthood), Catholic and Episcopal mass, Muslim ceremonies—such as salat (prayer five times a day) and sawm (fasting)—are all ceremonies performed to bring the sacred in to bless some kind of event.

I am only going to discuss one ceremony with you: the ceremony of forgiveness. We cannot be free from depression if we are filled with fear, anger, regret, and the desire for revenge against those who have hurt us. We don't have to forget, but we do have to forgive. If you read the Lord's Prayer carefully, you will see that our sins are not forgiven unless we forgive those who have sinned against us.

Forgiveness Ceremony

This is a personal ceremony that has been passed down to us by the Twisted Hairs of Turtle Island. The intent of the ceremony is to allow you to experience *dainishui*, which means "From my heart, I give away any and all animosity, resentment, grievance, indebtedness, hostility, and hate. This is erased forever from the circle of experience, and life is restored."

Procedure:

1. Find a tree willing to do the ceremony and offer the tree tobacco as thanks. You can also do this ceremony indoors with a potted plant.

2. Walk around the tree three times to align with the energy and prepare yourself for the dialogue. State with clear intent what you are there to accomplish and ask the tree for help.

3. Start with your back against the tree facing southeast and move around the tree in the order presented below.

4. Ask in each direction if there is any forgiveness of that type needed. Then listen actively to nature as you do. Your inner guidance will move your awareness to what needs to be forgiven. Focus *only* on forgiving yourself the first time around. Give away tobacco as needed or smoke a few puffs of a cigarette, and then leave the tobacco (not the paper or the filter). Then work the entire wheel again, this time focusing on forgiving others.

SE: Character Assault or Individuality Forgiveness

This direction has to do with perceiving that you have been attacked by someone or something (or yourself) in a way that blocked your expression of individuality. How did you shut down your shining? What mistakes did you make?

Mistakes are stepping-stones to excellence and mastery. If you cannot forgive yourself for these, you will never become totally empowered in yourself.

NW: Karmic Forgiveness

This is where you acknowledge that you are the author of your own book of life. Forgive yourself for the amount of pain, suffering, cruelty, and harshness you wrote into your book of life in order to learn. Forgive yourself for being ignorant of your self-pity and self-importance in equal measure, for holding on to old karmic patterns rather than taking the risk of trying new proactive patterns.

Forgive differences between your patterns and the patterns of others.

Forgive yourself for judging the way others learn even if they have chosen to learn the hard way.

Forgive yourself for judging the way you have refused what others have tried to give you.

Forgive yourself in all five aspects of your being (physical, mental, spiritual, emotional, and sexual) for the times and ways you were unwilling to accept life and avoided death and change even though you knew they were needed.

Forgive yourself for avoiding "going for the gold."

Forgive yourself for the inability to accept the death of others (anger, despair) who they left too soon, how they left, that you didn't say what you wanted to say before they left.

SW: Intrusion or Commitment Forgiveness

Blaming others always prevents us from forgiving ourselves. How did you do this to others? How did you interfere with their dream or life space? How did you sabotage your dream, violate your own space or life processes?

Forgive where there have been intrusions. Even if they intruded on you, what must you forgive yourself for?

How have you violated your commitments? Where, when, and with whom have you violated or broken agreements and contracts?

NE: Tyrant Stress Forgiveness

This is where we remember those people who were tyrants in our lives. We were unable to stand up to them and say "no." Instead, we become a victim. Forgive yourself for the times you did not stand up to them. Forgive yourself for the times you gave away the gift you carry, and it was not accepted by others; for when you were unable to communicate your ideals and principals; and when you lacked the physical skills or ability to protect yourself from violence, predators, and attacks on your spirit.

East: Betrayal Forgiveness

Betrayal includes attacks against the essence of your being—circumstances in which you were betrayed, and there was nothing you could do to stop it. You didn't allow it to happen; it happened despite everything you did to stop it.

Betrayal includes anything that crosses your innocent purity and is the deepest wound that requires forgiveness. It includes: sexual abuse, threats to your lifestyle (e.g., stolen life savings, reputation ruined), or corruption of a spiritual path (being misled spiritually). What part did you play in this? For what must you forgive yourself?

North: Parental Forgiveness

Forgiving your parents is the key to no longer identifying yourself as their child, recognizing you learned the lessons they gave you as parental image makers. Forgive yourself (and them) for any pain you may have experienced in the process of learning your karmic lesson.

Now look at your role as a parent. You may need to forgive yourself for:

- The decision to have children

- Choosing not to have more children

- Giving birth to a child with deformities

- Not parenting as you wish you had

- Judging or alienating your child

South: Partner/Significant Other Forgiveness

This covers any relationship where contracts were not kept between lovers, siblings, friends, or business associates. Forgiveness may also be needed for making poor agreements in the first place.[5]

Closing The Ceremony

When you have worked the wheel twice, once to forgive yourself and again to forgive others, you are ready to close your ceremony. Make your final giveaways (e.g., a thing you love, tobacco, a piece of your hair). Vow to keep the past in the past.

Give the tree water, a little plant food, hug the tree, and thank it.

Thank yourself for forgiving yourself and others to the best of your ability.

Walk into your life with a greater tolerance and a lighter heart.

---

5   This ceremony was gifted to me by Debbie Mast and comes from the Deer Tribe Sweet Medicine Sundance Tradition.

CHAPTER NINETEEN

Gratitude

Here are the words to a beautiful Quaker song.

> T'is a gift to be simple.
> T'is a gift to be free.
> T'is a gift to come down where we ought to be.
> And when we are in the place just right,
> we'll be in the garden of love and delight.
> When true simplicity is gained to bow and to bend
> we will not be ashamed.
> To turn and to turn t'will be our delight,
> 'til by turning, turning we come round right.

Lyrics: Joseph Brackett 1797–1882

My friend Eileen told me that when she began feeling angry and resentful of her paralysis, she was sliding down the slippery slope to the depression that she experienced during the first few years of her paralysis. The bottom of the slippery slope was the wish to be blotted out of existence and the inability to communicate with anyone. She would stop her slide by repeating the following mantra: "Grateful I am I can breathe. Grateful I am I can speak. Grateful I am that I can listen. Grateful I am that I can teach. Grateful I am for whipped cream and chocolate." She would repeat the mantra, adding to it the small things in life that she did not notice most of the time, until her heart began to overflow, and she was able to laugh at herself, becoming simpler and freer.

I am grateful to you, dear reader, for sharing this journey with me, this everyday journey from depression to light.

As we age, we become increasingly complicated. We are anything but simple or free. Yet, when we experience depression, we are stripped down to our bare essentials. If we allow ourselves to be transformed by the experience, we emerge with our life simplified and free from what is unnecessary and non-essential. The old Indian man, the old monk, and Woman Who Walks in Balance were transformed by life circumstances and depression. As they moved through and beyond depression, each one of them experienced a kind of freedom and simplicity that was totally new to them. The fruit of their experience was a kind of gratitude that moved closer to the love and light that is the heart of the universe.

Help and Protection for Your Journey

Do the work.

Walk your talk.

Trust in God and trust your "gut."

"By their fruits will you know them"
Matthew 7:16–20

Good teachers live upright
lives and walk their talk.

Speak the truth when you can.

Mind your own business

Walk away when you want to argue.

Choose to be happy.

Keep yourself in harmony
both within and without.

Work to be healthy.

Develop your sense of humor,
and use it as necessary.

Synchronicity

Synchronicity refers to events that are connected by seemingly meaningful coincidence rather than by cause and effect. On that note, I am going to end with something for you to consider.

One of the last people I saw as an analyst was a woman who was a physicist. I asked her once how she perceived the world around us, and she told me that she believed the entire universe functioned with synchronicity. I was astounded at her remark, and I felt as if the floor had dropped out from under me.

Think about it.

CPSIA information can be obtained
at www.ICGtesting.com
Printed in the USA
BVHW030017200720
584047BV00005B/226